Filmmakers

Other books in the History Makers series:

History MAKERS

Filmmakers

By Andy Koopmans

LUCENT BOOKS

An imprint of Thomson Gale, a part of The Thomson Corporation

THOMSON

GALE

Detroit • New York • San Francisco • San Diego • New Haven, Conn.
Waterville, Maine • London • Munich

To all the filmmakers who still believe in art

LIBRARY OF CONGRESS CATALOGING-IN-PUBLICATION DATA

Koopmans, Andy.
  Filmmakers / by Andy Koopmans.
    p. cm. — (History makers)
  Includes bibliographical references and index.
  ISBN 1-59018-598-6 (hard cover : alk. paper)
  1. Motion picture producers and directors—Biography—Juvenile literature. I. Title. II.
Series.
PN1998.2.K66 2004
791.4302'33'092273—dc22

                                                    2004012774

Printed in the United States of America

CONTENTS

FOREWORD

The literary form most often referred to as "multiple biography" was perfected in the first century A.D. by Plutarch, a perceptive and talented moralist and historian who hailed from the small town of Chaeronea in central Greece. His most famous work, *Parallel Lives*, consists of a long series of biographies of noteworthy ancient Greek and Roman statesmen and military leaders. Frequently, Plutarch compares a famous Greek to a famous Roman, pointing out similarities in personality and achievements. These expertly constructed and very readable tracts provided later historians and others, including playwrights like Shakespeare, with priceless information about prominent ancient personages and also inspired new generations of writers to tackle the multiple biography genre.

The Lucent History Makers series proudly carries on the venerable tradition handed down from Plutarch. Each volume in the series consists of a set of five to eight biographies of important and influential historical figures who were linked together by a common factor. In *Rulers of Ancient Rome*, for example, all the figures were generals, consuls, or emperors of either the Roman Republic or Empire; while the subjects of *Fighters Against American Slavery*, though they lived in different places and times, all shared the same goal, namely, the eradication of human servitude. Mindful that politicians and military leaders are not (and never have been) the only people who shape the course of history, the editors of the series have also included representatives from a wide range of endeavors, including scientists, artists, writers, philosophers, religious leaders, and sports figures.

Each book is intended to give a range of figures—some well known, others less known; some who made a great impact on history, others who made only a small impact. For instance, by making Columbus's initial voyage possible, Spain's Queen Isabella I, featured in *Women Leaders of Nations*, helped to open up the New World to exploration and exploitation by the European powers. Inarguably, therefore, she made a major contribution to a series of events that had momentous consequences for the entire world. By contrast, Catherine II, the eighteenth-century Russian queen, and Golda Meir, the modern Israeli prime minister, did not play roles of global impact; however, their policies and actions significantly influenced the historical development of both their own countries and their regional neighbors. Regardless of their relative importance in the greater historical scheme, all of the figures chronicled in the History Makers series made contributions to posterity; and their public achievements, as well as what is known about their private lives, are presented and evaluated in light of the most recent scholarship.

In addition, each volume in the series is documented and substantiated by a wide array of primary and secondary source quotations. The primary source quotes enliven the text by presenting eyewitness views of the times and culture in which each history maker lived, while the secondary source quotes, taken from the works of respected modern scholars, offer expert elaboration and/or critical commentary. Each quote is footnoted, demonstrating to the reader exactly where biographers find their information. The footnotes also provide the reader with the means of conducting additional research. Finally, to further guide and illuminate readers, each volume in the series features photographs, two bibliographies, and a comprehensive index.

The History Makers series provides both students engaged in research and more casual readers with informative, enlightening, and entertaining overviews of individuals from a variety of circumstances, professions, and backgrounds. No doubt all of them, whether loved or hated, benevolent or cruel, constructive or destructive, will remain endlessly fascinating to each new generation seeking to identify the forces that shaped their world.

Introduction

Hollywood Outsiders

One of the most important struggles in filmmaking is between art and money. While all media are in some way intertwined with commerce, filmmaking has always been an expensive financial venture, requiring special equipment and materials, facilities, and often a host of specialists, from casting directors and cinematographers to key grips and sound editors. Millions of dollars—often tens or hundreds of millions of dollars—are required to make most feature films today, and without independent wealth, filmmakers have always been beholden to their investors, most often the big Hollywood studios. Most of these studios, who control an enormous percentage of the film production in the world, are controlled by businesspeople and owned by multinational corporations that are frequently less willing to risk millions of dollars on filmmakers' creative innovations. Thus, although filmmaking is both an art and a business, Hollywood studios tend to treat it more like the latter.

The Studio System

In the early part of the twentieth century, the so-called studio system had a near monopoly on cinema. Studios were all-in-one shops staffed with scriptwriters, actors, directors, and all others required to make films. The studios also owned their own theaters in which they could show the films they made.

Like assembly line automobile manufacturing factories, their goal was to produce as many films as inexpensively as possible at the highest profit possible. Between the 1920s and 1940s, during the period known as the studio system's golden age, studios were often able to produce several films a week. The bulk of these films were of poor quality and did not stand the test of time; however, the few that were popular brought in so much money that they paid for themselves and the cost of the less popular films. As film historian Thomas Schatz believes, the Hollywood studio system was run in such a way that the style and artistic expression of studio films were influenced more by the power system of the studio than by the director.

Between the 1920s and 1940s, large Hollywood studios like Paramount Pictures produced a huge number of low-budget films, sometimes at the rate of several films per week.

The structure of the Hollywood studio system has changed since the 1940s; however, the Hollywood film industry is still dominated by the major studios, and their goal of profit remains primary. Like the old golden era, today the studios are predominantly helmed by businesspeople, not filmmakers. Filmmakers who work with the studios and want to try artistically or commercially risky ideas often find themselves opposed by teams of business people.

Creative Control

Since the beginning of filmmaking, however, there have been filmmakers who have sought and achieved either financial independence from the studio system or enough of a reputation to gain creative control over their work within that system. This control has enabled them to create films that have had a significant impact on the history of cinema. They are not alone. From the inception of filmmaking as a popular entertainment media, there have been numerous maverick filmmakers whose independence, talent, and artistic vision have shaped cinema. These filmmakers have strived to make films that are not only commercially appealing but also of artistic innovation and importance. The five profiled in this book—Alfred Hitchcock, Stanley Kubrick, Francis Ford Coppola, Spike Lee, and Peter Jackson—are selected from those numbers.

The filmmakers in this volume were outsiders to the studio system for one reason or another—by choice or by circumstance. Each strived for total creative control over his work, each was willing to take large risks for the sake of creativity, and each strived to work with a maximum degree of independence.

CHAPTER 1

Alfred Hitchcock

Few directors have contributed so much to the cinema in quantity and quality as Alfred Hitchcock. During a career spanning six decades he directed fifty-four films, rarely resting more than a few weeks between projects. While the sheer volume of his work alone was remarkable, Hitchcock also developed and refined a cinematic style unmistakably his own, which has been enjoyed, studied, and imitated more than that of perhaps any director in history.

Critics have argued that because Hitchcock was so devoted to his career and because it took up so much of his life, to study his films is to study Hitchcock himself. His official biographer, John Russell Taylor, once remarked, "Hitchcock is not so much in his films: he *is* his films."[1]

Loner

Alfred Joseph Hitchcock was born on August 13, 1899, in Leytonstone, at the time a growing burgh twenty miles northeast of London. The third child of William Hitchcock, a grocer, and his wife, Emma, he grew up living above the family's stores in various places around London's East End. Several years younger than his siblings William Jr., born in 1890, and Ellen, born in 1892, Alfred spent much of his childhood playing alone and was generally a timid and well-behaved child. Additionally, from early childhood he was overweight, a condition that would make him self-conscious for the rest of his life.

The Hitchcocks were a middle-class, devoutly Catholic family. William and Emma Hitchcock instilled discipline and a strong work ethic in their children. Sent to Catholic school for most of his education, Alfred worked hard, was an average student, and stayed out of trouble, but took no great pleasure in school. Because of his aloofness and weight, other children thought he was strange, and he spent most of his school years as a loner.

However, in his solitude, Hitchcock had an eager imagination and sense of exploration and found numerous ways to entertain himself. He spent many hours reading, letting the books take him to other places and other times. He enjoyed riding buses to

Alfred Hitchcock developed a unique cinematic style that helped establish him as one of the most important filmmakers of all time.

explore the city and also plotted out elaborate imaginary world excursions using maps and ship and train timetables.

Despite their strictness, Hitchcock's parents were also very kind and loving toward their children. Emma Hitchcock devoted herself to raising her children, and their father spent as much time with them as possible, often taking them to cultural events, particularly the theater, for which Alfred developed an early passion. His love of theater was eventually rivaled by that of motion pictures, which at the time were a new phenomenon, the first film having been exhibited in 1895. One of the first films Hitchcock remembers seeing was *A Ride on a Runaway Train*, which gave the viewer the thrill of speeding through scenic landscapes on the front of a moving train. Film became an obsession to Hitchcock, and he began reading trade magazines about the new medium, learning as much as possible about how films were made.

Finding the Cinema

Despite his early interest in movies, Hitchcock's path from childhood to filmmaker was indirect. In 1913 when he left school at fourteen, a typical age for leaving school at the time, he wanted to become an engineer. He enrolled in classes at the University of London to study the discipline, but a year later his father died after a period of ill health and Hitchcock took a job as a clerk at the Henley Telegraph and Cable Company to help support his family.

World War I broke out that same year. Too young to enlist, Hitchcock instead returned to the University of London to take evening classes. The tedium of his job led him to study subjects that interested him, including art, where he learned to sketch. Drawing became one of his favorite pastimes, and his supervisors at Henley soon recognized his skill. They transferred him to the advertising department, where he employed his new skills and imagination by publishing a monthly magazine for Henley employees. As the editor and chief contributor of the magazine, he drew cartoons and artwork and wrote several short stories for publication.

Then, in 1919, Hitchcock's creative urge led him for the first time into the movie industry. He was hired by Paramount Studios to write title cards for a movie called *The Sorrows of Satan*. These

Hitchcock views a drawing by surrealist painter Salvador Dali (second from right). Hitchcock always incorporated startling visual imagery into his films.

cards were used in silent films to convey dialogue and plot. The studio was impressed with his work, and although the production of *The Sorrows of Satan* was canceled, the studio hired Hitchcock to title its next project, a film called *The Great Day*. He worked during his off-hours from Henley's, and the film was such a success—largely because of Hitchcock's contribution—that the producers eventually hired him full-time, which allowed him to quit the telegraph equipment office.

Rising Through the Ranks

Working at Paramount Studios was a great learning experience for Hitchcock. Although his job involved plenty of hard work, the atmosphere of the studio was informal, and Hitchcock, originally hired as a title designer, soon found himself performing other tasks around the studio. He worked in many capacities—as office boy, art director, and finally director, filling in to shoot a few scenes for a film called *Always Tell Your Wife*. He was so good at directing that he was given the chance to direct a short film called *Number 13*; however, before it was finished, the studio's British branch went out of business in 1923.

Nonetheless, Hitchcock's abilities and talent were so valued that he was one of the few people at Paramount to be hired by the new owners, Michael Balcon and Victor Seville. These men were British producers making films for C.M. Woolf, a well-known film distributor. The first film Hitchcock worked on for the new producers was *Woman to Woman*. For the film, Hitchcock worked in several capacities, including as art director and screenwriter.

Alma

Woman to Woman also gave Hitchcock his first opportunity to work with a young woman named Alma Lucy Reville. Born exactly one day after Hitchcock, Reville was a London native who had started working in films at the age of sixteen. Reville had years of experience as producer and editor at the studio. Although they had worked in the same studio for three years, they had barely spoken to each other until the production of *Woman to Woman*. Hitchcock had noticed her and thought she was attractive, but he was still quite shy, particularly around women, and had never been on a date before.

Hitchcock and Reville got to know each other well during the film production and worked together on several other films over the next year. Then, in 1923, while they were on a ship returning

Hitchcock poses with his wife, Alma Lucy Reville, in New York in 1938. The two were wed in 1926 after a three-year engagement.

to England from continental Europe after an assignment there, Hitchcock proposed. Not confident about what her response would be, Hitchcock asked Reville when she was seasick so she might be less inclined to say no. He wrote that in response, Reville "groaned, nodded her head, and burped."[2]

Because he wanted to establish himself as a director first, Hitchcock and Reville did not set an immediate wedding date. He recalled: "I had wanted to become, first, a movie director and, second, Alma's husband—not in order of preference, to be sure, but because I felt the bargaining power implicit in the first was necessary in obtaining the second."[3]

Influences

The next film Hitchcock worked on, *The Blackguard*, was shot on location in Germany, which at the time was home to some of the most renowned directors in Europe, including Fritz Lang and F.W. Murnau. During off-hours, Hitchcock spent time on the set of Murnau's latest film, *The Last Laugh*, learning techniques that would later influence his own directing style. Among these were creative ways of manipulating the camera angles to create dramatic effects and means of creating illusions on film. Perhaps most important, Hitchcock saw that Murnau eschewed the use of title cards in his film because he wanted to tell the entire story without

Actor Paul Newman and Hitchcock watch a rehearsal on the set of Torn Curtain. *Hitchcock preferred filming on studio sets instead of working on location.*

words. This notion became profoundly important to Hitchcock, and for the rest of his career, even into the sound era, Hitchcock insisted that films were primarily visual and that the story should be told as much as possible in images.

Hitchcock was able to use some of his new film techniques and ideas soon after returning from Germany when Balcon asked him to direct a feature-length film. Hitchcock was pleased but surprised. "Quite seriously, I had never thought of being a director. I was too darned busy on the job."[4] However, he felt ready and readily took the opportunity.

First Film

Filmed in 1925, Hitchcock's first feature film was called *The Pleasure Garden.* A melodrama about two chorus girls involving infidelity, corruption, and murder, much of the film was shot on location (that is, not in a studio but at real places) in Germany and Italy. The location shooting proved to be a comedy of errors. While the cast and crew traveled around Europe to film, equipment was lost, customs officials seized ten thousand feet of unexposed film that Hitchcock had tried to smuggle over the border to save on the import tax, and the money for the film production was stolen out of Hitchcock's hotel room in Italy, leaving him with no money to finish the film. Fortunately, Hitchcock was able to borrow enough funds from various people, including his leading actress, to complete filming. From then on, however, Hitchcock always preferred working in a studio where he could control everything. This need to exercise control over his films as much as possible was something for which Hitchcock would become renowned during his career.

After *The Pleasure Garden*, at Balcon's request Hitchcock immediately directed a second film, also in Germany, called *The Mountain Eagle*. Although he was still learning his craft and was not entirely happy with either film, Hitchcock was disappointed when he returned to England to learn that Woolf did not like the artistic touches that Hitchcock had picked up from Murnau. Woolf decided not to release either film, which was a blow to Hitchcock, who worried that his career as a director was over before it had barely started.

The Lodger

Within a few weeks, Hitchcock's worries about his career were alleviated when Balcon asked him to direct a third film, based on a novel inspired by the Jack the Ripper murders. Jack the Ripper was the nickname given to a never-captured murderer responsible for a series of brutal killings in 1888 in the town of Whitechapel, not far from where Hitchcock had grown up. Fascinated by crime as a child and young man, and well versed in Ripper lore, Hitchcock welcomed the chance to work on a film and accepted the offer from Balcon.

Hitchcock finished the film in less than three months. Called *The Lodger*, the film is set in London during a streak of murders of blonde prostitutes, similar to the crimes in Whitechapel in 1888.

When *The Lodger* was finished, Woolf thought the film was dreadful and refused to release it. However, after some minor editing and reshooting, Balcon presented the film to a group of critics who exuberantly praised it. One critic called it "the finest British production ever made."[5] Faced with such response, Woolf released it to great success in 1926 and then released Hitchcock's first two films the following year. Although the other films did not do as well, *The Lodger* received such acclaim that, at the age of twenty-five, Hitchcock became recognized as the most promising director in the country.

The Hitchcocks

Hitchcock's newfound success allowed him the financial confidence to finally marry Reville, more than three years after he had proposed. They wed in a small ceremony on December 2, 1926, and settled into an apartment in West London.

Reville, who many said would have gone on to be a talented director had she not married, instead became Hitchcock's most valued and trusted associate and collaborator. Over the years of their marriage she would be involved in some capacity for most of his films, with or without credit. The two settled into a comfortable and harmonious marriage. As wealthy and famous as Hitchcock would ever become, he and his wife lived a fairly normal middle-class life, putting on few airs. Hitchcock later said, "I never felt any desire to move out of my own class."[6] He kept regular working hours, always making time for home life, particularly after the birth of their first and only child, Patricia Alma Hitchcock, who was born July 7, 1928.

The First Talkie

While he settled into family life, Hitchcock continued to hone his skills by working on more silent films. Lured away from Balcon's studio by British International Pictures (BIP) with promise of larger production budgets and more creative freedom, Hitchcock made three films in quick succession: *The Ring* (1927), *The Farmer's Wife* (1928), and *Champagne* (1928).

Despite his prolific output, none of his films since *The Lodger* did as well critically or commercially. However, his fourth film for

Hitchcock's wife (right) was involved with most of the director's films in some capacity. Here, the two collaborate on a film script.

After the 1927 release of the first talkie, The Jazz Singer *(pictured),*
Hitchcock remade Blackmail *using sound.*

BIP, *Blackmail* (1929), provided him with a unique opportunity
and challenge. In Hollywood in 1927, *The Jazz Singer* was released as the first ever sound film, also known as a "talkie."
Hitchcock recognized that sound films were the future. He later
wrote: "I was convinced that talkies were no mere flash in the
pan, and that the days of silent film had passed."[7] Although he
had originally filmed *Blackmail* as a silent film, he asked BIP for
the money to remake the film as a talkie. His producers agreed,
and *Blackmail* became Britain's first full-length feature sound film,
drawing huge audiences.

Ups and Downs

Over the next four years, Hitchcock continued his work at BIP, directing numerous films, but he had little or no personal investment
in them, as most were uninspired assignments from the studio.
Bored, Hitchcock finished his contract and left BIP in 1933 to
work for London Film Productions, a new and promising film
company. However, the studio was in financial difficulty and after
a year of working on a project that never got funded, Hitchcock

Actors Leslie Banks (left) and Nova Pilbeam perform a scene from the 1934 Hitchcock thriller The Man Who Knew Too Much. *Hitchcock referred to this film as the true start to his career.*

left. Desperate to work after what was for him an unusually long period without directing a film, he worked on a film called *Waltzes from Vienna* with an independent producer. Unfortunately, Hitchcock ended up hating the film, calling it "my lowest ebb."[8]

However, while shooting *Waltzes*, Hitchcock became reacquainted with Michael Balcon, who had become head of a new studio called Gaumont British Pictures. The two decided to work together again, this time on an adaptation of a popular spy novel. It was Hitchcock's seventeenth feature film, and he called it *The Man Who Knew Too Much* (1934). Since *The Lodger* it was his most important film, the one he later called "the real start of my career."[9] Well received, it was the first in a series of successful spy thrillers that included *The 39 Steps* (1935), *Secret Agent* (1936), and *Sabotage* (1936). In each, Hitchcock creatively established dramatic tension, suspense, and intrigue, and the films marked the zenith of Hitchcock's career in Britain, establishing his reputation internationally.

Critics later argued that in this series of films were the seeds of his most successful work to come. They bore themes and traits that would become Hitchcock hallmarks. For instance, in *The 39 Steps* Hitchcock for the first time used a narrative device that he called a MacGuffin, named after a purposefully nonsensical Scottish joke. In Hitchcock's films, a MacGuffin is a story element that everyone in a film thinks is important but that matters little to the audience. In *The 39 Steps*, the MacGuffin is secret government plans for a new warplane. Most of the characters in the film are driven to get their hands on the secret; however, for the purpose of the story the plans mean little. The MacGuffin could just as well have been a satchel of diamonds or a suitcase of money. The real story of the film from the audience's perspective is the suspense and humor in the main character's interactions with others as he is pursued across Europe by spies and the police.

Looking Across the Ocean

Hitchcock's films received positive press and attention both in Europe and in the United States, and by the late 1930s, he had received numerous offers from Hollywood studios that wanted him to come to the States to work for them. Hitchcock had never been to America before, but he had fantasized about doing so since he was a child. Although he loved England and was comfortable there, he knew that the American film industry had much to offer that the British industry did not—particularly larger production budgets that would allow him more creative freedom. Film had become his life, and he felt compelled to go where he could make the best movies. Hitchcock accepted an offer from David O. Selznick, head of Selznick International Pictures, to work as a director on staff.

America

After the Hitchcocks' arrival in Los Angeles, Hitchcock began work on his first American film, *Rebecca*, an adaptation of a Daphne Du Maurier novel, ironically set in England and cast with mostly British actors. From the beginning of the project, Selznick intruded on Hitchcock's work, appearing regularly on the set to critique what was going on. By the end of the filming, the director and producer were so annoyed with each other that Hitchcock was concerned that he might not be able to work with Selznick after all. However, Selznick's faith in Hitchcock was renewed when the picture opened to rave reviews and large audiences, and he agreed to leave the director alone to his work from then on.

Rebecca went on to win eleven Academy Award nominations for 1940, receiving the most prestigious Best Picture Award; however,

Best Picture awards go to the producer, not the director, so Hitchcock missed his first opportunity at an award. This pattern would last his entire career—despite the acclaim for his pictures, he would never win an Oscar.

The War Years

Back in England, the war with Germany was heating up. Bombing raids over the country were expected, and Hitchcock worried about his family, particularly his mother, who still lived in London. He tried to persuade her to join him in America, but she refused to leave England. However, to keep her safer, Hitchcock did persuade her to move to the countryside to a cottage he owned.

Despite his efforts to protect her, Hitchcock's mother's health failed and she died in 1942, before the war was over; additionally, his brother William's business was destroyed in the war and he later committed suicide. Hitchcock was busy working and could not attend the funerals of either family member, but he made a visit to England in 1943. He was distraught by the devastation that the bombings had brought to the country.

Hitchcock, his wife, their daughter Patricia, and a production assistant (far right) arrive in Hollywood. There, Hitchcock began work on the critically acclaimed Rebecca.

Cary Grant (left) and Ingrid Bergman became close friends with Hitchcock during the production of Notorious *(pictured), the director's most famous war film.*

Although he was an expatriate in America, Hitchcock was patriotic and made several films during the war years, from 1940 to 1945, which dealt either thematically or directly with the war. Among these were *Foreign Correspondent*, *Saboteur*, and *Lifeboat*. The best received among his war films was *Notorious*. The film involved a confusing Nazi spy plot—a MacGuffin dealing with Nazis smuggling uranium to create weapons. The film became a Hitchcock classic because of the direction and the on-screen chemistry between the two lead actors, Cary Grant and Ingrid Bergman, both of whom became close friends and favorite associates of Hitchcock's.

During this same period, he made more personal films, including one that remained a favorite of his, *Shadow of a Doubt*, which involved murder and suspense coming into the life of a family living in the small northern California town of Santa Rosa. During the filming, much of which took place in Santa Rosa, Hitchcock fell in love with the area and bought a Spanish cottage near Santa Cruz.

Independence

In 1948, desiring complete control over his work, Hitchcock set up his own production company, Transatlantic Pictures, with Sidney Bernstein, an old friend and associate of Hitchcock's in London.

Together, they produced two films, *Rope* and *Under Capricorn*. In *Rope*, Hitchcock created a technical challenge for himself. He decided to shoot the film like a stage play, using unusually lengthy shots, some lasting up to ten minutes, and hiding the cuts between the shots so that the film seems to unfold as one continuous scene. Hitchcock later said that he undertook the film as a self-indulgent stunt and considered it an interesting failure; however, because of its technical innovation it received good press and reviews and made a small profit for his new company. Unfortunately, *Under Capricorn*, a nineteenth-century costume drama set in Australia and shot in England, was a costly failure that Hitchcock always regretted. It was so costly that Hitchcock and Bernstein had to shut down Transatlantic Pictures.

Golden Era

Hitchcock had no trouble finding work again, as he remained a sought-after talent in Europe and America. He took a contract with Warner Brothers as director-producer for four films. Of the four, three were suspense thrillers of varying success. The two most successful and enduring from the period were *Strangers on a Train* and *Dial M for Murder*.

In the 1950s, many in the movie business worried about the encroachment of the popularity of television on the film industry. Hitchcock had nothing to fear from television. In fact, he chose to get involved with it. Striking a deal with the television studio CBS, Hitchcock developed a half-hour suspense thriller and mystery television program called *Alfred Hitchcock Presents*. The show ran from 1955 to 1962 and then changed to an hour-long program as *The Alfred Hitchcock Hour*, running from 1962 to 1965. Although he directed only twenty of the over three hundred episodes broadcast over the years, Hitchcock appeared before each show, often humorously dressed in a costume related to that night's story, to introduce the program. Hitchcock delivered humorous and often mischievous monologues straight-faced, and these appearances made him one of the most recognized faces in show business.

Behind the movie camera, Hitchcock was equally successful in the 1950s and 1960s. Critically acclaimed as Hitchcock's golden era, during this period he produced several of his most critically and commercially enduring and popular suspense thriller masterpieces, including *Rear Window*, *To Catch a Thief*, a remake of his 1930s classic *The Man Who Knew Too Much*, *North by Northwest*, *Vertigo*, *Psycho*, and *The Birds*. These films were the

Actress Janet Leigh screams during the famous shower scene from Psycho. *Many critics consider* Psycho *to be the most influential horror film in history.*

climactic payoff of three decades of experimentation, technical innovation, and development of style. In them, Hitchcock created what would become some of cinema's favorite and infamous screen moments.

Perhaps the best known of all of Hitchcock's films was *Psycho*, a film that according to Steven Jay Schneider has been called "the most influential horror film in history."[10] Hitchcock had challenged himself to make a low-budget horror film, and he succeeded in making a classic. In one of cinema's most famous scenes, the heroine, played by actress Janet Leigh, is brutally stabbed to death in a shower. The forty-five-second scene required seven days, seventy different camera setups, and ninety editing cuts and was the pinnacle of Hitchcock's technical and editing achievements.

Filmography of Alfred Hitchcock

Family Plot (1976)	Mr. & Mrs. Smith (1941)
Frenzy (1972)	Foreign Correspondent (1940)
Topaz (1969)	Rebecca (1940)
Torn Curtain (1966)	Jamaica Inn (1939)
Marnie (1964)	Lady Vanishes, The (1938)
Birds, The (1963)	Young and Innocent (1937)
Psycho (1960)	Sabotage (1936)
North by Northwest (1959)	Secret Agent (1936)
Vertigo (1958)	39 Steps, The (1935)
"Suspicion" (1957) TV Series	The Man Who Knew Too Much (1934)
Wrong Man, The (1956)	Waltzes from Vienna (1933)
Man Who Knew Too Much, The (1956)	Number Seventeen (1932)
Trouble with Harry, The (1955)	Rich and Strange (1932)
To Catch a Thief (1955)	Skin Game, The (1931)
Rear Window (1954)	Elastic Affair, An (1930)
Dial M for Murder (1954)	Elstree Calling (1930)
I Confess (1953)	Juno and the Paycock (1930)
Strangers on a Train (1951)	Murder! (1930)
Stage Fright (1950)	Sound Test for Blackmail (1929)
Under Capricorn (1949)	Manxman, The (1929)
Rope (1948)	Blackmail (1929)
Paradine Case, The (1947)	Champagne (1928)
Notorious (1946)	Farmer's Wife, The (1928)
Spellbound (1945)	Easy Virtue (1928)
Bon Voyage (1944)	Downhill (1927)
Lifeboat (1944)	Ring, The (1927)
Shadow of a Doubt (1943)	Lodger, The (1927)
Saboteur (1942)	Mountain Eagle, The (1926)
Suspicion (1941)	Pleasure Garden, The (1925)

Last Years

In the late 1960s and early 1970s, Hitchcock's career went into decline. Although he was in his sixties and seventies and had no financial need to continue to work, he gave no thought to quitting. When asked what kept him going, he said "I think you have a sort of instinct which pushes you towards what you can do best, and once you have found it, it becomes a habit to keep on doing it."[11]

Despite his determination to continue to work, his health and that of his wife, Alma—who suffered two strokes in the early 1970s—slowed his production. Among a number of maladies, he suffered from severe arthritis, which he self-medicated with increasing amounts of alcohol. Additionally, his next few films were a string of disappointments, the exception being *Frenzy*, made in England and released in 1972.

Nonetheless, during these years Hitchcock's prestige was never higher. While he had often garnered good reviews over the years both in America and abroad, his work had mostly been seen as mere entertainment. However, during this period Hitchcock became recognized by international scholars and film connoisseurs. His work was studied for its technical and stylistic achievements, particularly among the critics-turned-filmmakers of the 1960s French cinema, who championed Hitchcock as one of the great geniuses of the medium.

Hitchcock also received official recognition for his achievements, both in England and in America. Although his movies had won numerous awards, Hitchcock had never won an Oscar for his directing. However, in 1968, he received the prestigious Irving G. Thalberg Memorial Award from the Academy of Motion Pictures, which is given periodically to filmmakers whose body of work is of a consistently high quality. Ten years later, Queen Elizabeth II bestowed a knighthood on Hitchcock, and he received the Lifetime Achievement Award from the American Film Institute in March 1979.

Although he attempted to keep working, soon after receiving his Lifetime Achievement Award, Hitchcock realized that he had neither the health nor the energy to continue directing. Hitchcock retired to his home in Bel Air with his wife, and on the morning of April 29, 1980, died quietly at the age of eighty.

Hitchcock's Legacy

Decades after his death, Hitchcock's work continues to inspire, inform, and serve as a source of entertainment. Although his work was already studied by film scholars before his death, in the years since his death he has become among the most written about and studied directors in history. Countless works of scholarship and appreciation have been written on his films and his work. Hitchcock's films continue to influence filmmakers who work in the suspense thriller genre, which he popularized and defined.

In recent years, restored versions of Hitchcock's classics have become very popular, in movie theaters and on DVD, and Hitchcock's entire collection of thrillers remains popular selections at video stores and on cable television. Moreover, Hitchcock himself is remembered and celebrated as the as-yet-unrivaled Master of Suspense.

CHAPTER 2

Stanley Kubrick

While most film directors of his generation worked their way through established studios, Stanley Kubrick was a completely self-taught filmmaker. He developed cinematographic expertise through photography (also self-taught) and obsessive film viewing, and figuring the rest out through reading and hands-on experience. Similarly, Kubrick learned about producing by raising money for his first films, establishing a preference for working independently of the studios. This made him one of the first successful independent filmmakers at the time.

During his career, Kubrick's film style, his preference for dark themes, and his innovations in visual storytelling made his work legendary. Although he produced only thirteen feature-length films over four and a half decades, several of them have been recognized as among the most daring, influential, and important films in the history of cinema. Meanwhile, his eccentric personality and extremely private, reclusive nature late in life made him a figure of speculation around whom rumors circulate, even after his death.

Childhood

Stanley Kubrick was born July 26, 1928, in New York City, the first of two children of Jacques "Jack" L. Kubrick MD, a general practitioner, and his wife, Gertrude Perveler Kubrick. Two years after Kubrick was born, the couple had a second child, a daughter, Barbara. The family of four lived for all of Kubrick's childhood and adolescence in the borough of the Bronx.

From childhood, Kubrick displayed many of the traits that would mark his personality for the rest of his life: He was quiet and shy but was also smart, serious, and curious about everything. In spite of his intelligence, in school Kubrick was a poor student, receiving bad grades because of poor attendance, and low marks for social behavior.

Concerned about his son's lack of interest in school, Kubrick's father tried to engage him in other activities. He taught Kubrick to play chess and bought him a professional-grade Graflex brand

Some critics regard the films of self-taught director Stanley Kubrick as among the most innovative in cinematic history.

camera, the same kind used by newspaper photographers at the time. Kubrick took up both chess and photography with a passion, becoming particularly obsessed with the latter. He carried his camera with him everywhere, often hiding it in a shopping bag with a hole cut around the lens so he could take photos of people without their knowing it.

As a teenager, Kubrick attended William Howard Taft High School. As in his earlier years, he had poor attendance and school did not interest him. "I never learned anything at school," he later said, "and I didn't read a book for pleasure until I was nineteen years old."[12]

Instead of going to class, Kubrick often attended the cinema, watching ten to twelve films a week. During this time, he first thought about making films. He remembered, "I'd keep seeing lousy films and saying to myself, 'I don't know anything about movie making, but I *couldn't* do anything worse than this.'"[13]

Photographer

Kubrick continued developing his photographic skills during his teen years, eventually becoming very sophisticated in his ability. Then, in 1944, when Kubrick was seventeen, President Franklin D. Roosevelt died, and Kubrick took a candid photograph of a grief-stricken New York newspaper vendor surrounded by headlines announcing the news. The photo so poignantly captured the emotion of the day that he was able to sell it for twenty-five dollars to a popular national magazine called *Look*. The art editor was so impressed by Kubrick's work that she hired him as a part-time photographer for the magazine. When he graduated from high school the following year, his grades were so poor that he could not get into college, so he took a full-time position with the magazine. The job provided him with a good salary and was an education in itself. "It was a miraculous break for me to get this job after graduation from high school," he later said, "not only because I learned a lot about photography, but also because it gave me a quick education in how things happened in the world."[14]

Two years later, Kubrick married Toba Metz, his high school girlfriend. Metz was seventeen and Kubrick nineteen when they married and moved into their own place, an apartment in the Greenwich Village neighborhood of New York City in lower Manhattan, renowned as a haven for young artists.

For the next three years, Kubrick worked on numerous assignments for *Look*, taking photos of celebrities and people on the street, and creating photo essays in which he would tell a story through a series of captioned photographs.

First Short Films

In 1950, while working for *Look*, Kubrick heard through a friend that the Time, Inc. company, one of the world's largest media companies, would pay up to $40,000 for a ten-minute short film

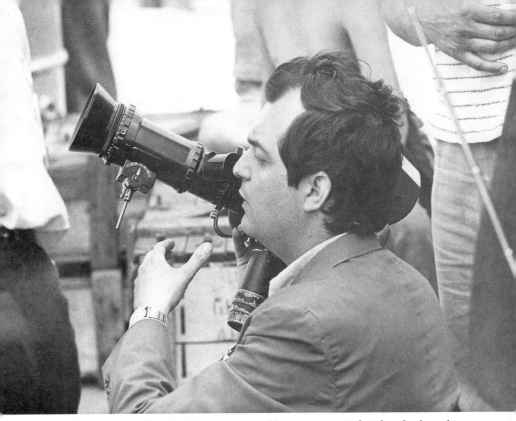

Kubrick uses a handheld camera to film a scene. Kubrick relied on his experience as a still photographer to help make his first short films.

to show in theaters as part of their *March of Time* weekly newsreel series. Although he had no experience, he was confident he could produce and direct a film of that length for only $1,500. With two high school friends working as his crew, Kubrick shot a film called *Day of the Fight*, a ten-minute short documenting the activities of a prizefighter named Walter Cartier who had been a subject of one of Kubrick's earlier photo essays for *Look*.

Despite his age and inexperience, Kubrick earned the respect of those who worked with him from the start. Cartier recalled, "Stanley was a very stoic, impassive but imaginative type person. . . . He commanded respect in a quiet, shy way. Whatever he wanted, you complied, he just captivated you. Anybody who worked with Stanley just did what Stanley wanted."[15]

Through his photographic experience, Kubrick had gained the ability to tell a story through still images and the talent carried over to motion pictures. Those who saw *Day of the Fight* thought the film was visually sophisticated, especially for a documentary. However, he had been overly optimistic about the cost. *Day of the Fight* cost $3,900 to make, and when it was done, Time, Inc., could not buy it because they had discontinued their *March of Time* series in 1951 due to rising costs. However, Kubrick was able to sell the film to another company, RKO-Pathé, who paid him $4,000. Although he made only $100, the film was released in 1951 as a part of a film series called *This Is America*. Kubrick was on his way as a filmmaker.

Over the next months, Kubrick made two other short films. One was a documentary called *The Flying Padre*, which followed the life of a priest who visited the members of his parish in the south-western United States via his own small single-engine plane. The other, *The Seafarers*, was a publicity film paid for by the Seafarers International Union, a group representing merchant marines.

Independent Filmmaker

In 1951, Kubrick quit his job at *Look* to become a full-time film-maker. Kubrick wanted to have creative control over his films, which meant finding investors to produce them. For his first film, he budgeted $40,000 and raised the money from family and friends, including a $30,000 investment from a wealthy uncle.

Kubrick's first film was *Fear and Desire,* a World War II film, one of three combat films he would make during his career. He later said his attraction to war as a subject was the inherent drama

Pictured is a scene from Kubrick's first film, Fear and Desire, *a project he completed on a shoestring budget of $40,000.*

of the soldier's life. "The soldier," he said, "is absorbing because all the circumstances surrounding him have a kind of charged intensity. For all its horror, war is pure drama, probably because it is one of the few remaining situations where men stand up for and speak up for what they believe to be their principles."[16]

Kubrick collaborated with high school friend Howard O. Sackler on the screenplay, which told the story of four soldiers stuck behind enemy lines in Europe after their plane is shot down. During their struggle to get to safety, the men take a young German woman hostage. The climax occurs when one of the men tries to rape the hostage and is shot by his fellow soldier.

Kubrick shot the film in February and March 1951 in Los Angeles, California, with a small crew and a rented camera. After several months of postproduction work, Kubrick had trouble selling the film to a distributor because of the dark subject matter. However, in 1953, an independent producer, Joseph Burstyn, screened the film and agreed to distribute it. The film was sold as a sexy B movie, and disappeared soon after it was released in March.

Kubrick looked back on the film with some embarrassment, saying it was "a very inept and pretentious effort"[17] but that it was a learning experience. Nonetheless, despite its B-movie packaging, it received some very strong reviews from those who recognized Kubrick's talent as a cinematographer.

Making Films Undercover

Soon after the release of *Fear and Desire*, Kubrick divorced his first wife and moved in with a dancer named Ruth Sobotka with whom he had been having an affair for some time. The couple married in 1955.

While preparing his next film, Kubrick continued his self-taught film school, seeing every movie he could. Sobotka recalled, "He was obsessed with going to see every film . . . [it] was all he really wanted to do."[18]

Kubrick opened his own film company called Minotaur Productions and again borrowed money from friends and relatives for his second feature, a dark-themed film noir–style movie called *Killer's Kiss*, written with his *Fear and Desire* writing partner, Sackler. Money was tight, so Kubrick filmed *Killer's Kiss* in a small studio and in the streets of New York. However, because the city required expensive filming permits to shoot outdoors, Kubrick filmed illegally, hiding the camera from view while actors played their roles in public unbeknownst to others on the streets. Despite this technique, the film went over budget by more than

$20,000. Fortunately, to cover the debt, Kubrick sold the film distribution rights to United Artists. This was a major achievement for an amateur independent filmmaker at the time.

Harris-Kubrick

Killer's Kiss did not make Kubrick a profit, and he was unable to repay his investors. However, in 1955 Kubrick met James B. Harris, a young film producer who was professionally and personally impressed with Kubrick. Harris recalled Kubrick as "the most intelligent, most creative person I had ever come in contact with."[19]

The two young men formed a friendship and a production company called Harris-Kubrick. In the partnership, Harris would produce Kubrick's films, and they would share the profits. Their first project together was the crime film *The Killing*, which Kubrick and crime novelist Jim Thompson adapted from a book by Lionel White.

When the film was released in 1956, it was a critical success. Many critics hailed Kubrick as the next Orson Welles, who had become a legend at age twenty-six with *Citizen Kane*. However, at the same time he received professional accolades, he suffered the failure of his second marriage. He and Ruth Kubrick divorced later that year.

Kubrick's First Controversy

Harris-Kubrick's second project was *Paths of Glory*, a World War I drama about three French army soldiers unjustly executed by the army for cowardice after their unit failed to perform an impossible mission ordered by a cynical careerist general.

Kubrick worked again with Jim Thompson to develop a screenplay while Harris brokered a deal with Metro Goldwyn Mayer (MGM) to produce and distribute the film. However, the deal fell through, putting the project in jeopardy. Fortunately, Kirk Douglas, one of Hollywood's most famous actors and an admirer of Kubrick's films, offered to star in the film and persuade United Artists to produce the film. Harris-Kubrick accepted.

Shot in Munich, Germany, *Paths of Glory* was a challenging film to direct. Kubrick worked hard to manage a cast of several hundred actors and extras and to re-create a realistic trench warfare battle. Additionally, once the film was released in 1957, controversy over the film arose because of the unfavorable portrayal of French army officers. Many reacted badly to the film, saying it was insulting and offensive to the French. The French government discouraged its citizens from seeing it, and Swiss and U.S. military banned it from being shown to troops.

Kubrick talks with Laurence Olivier on the set of Spartacus *in 1959. Dismayed by the difficulties involved in making the film, Kubrick vowed never again to work in Hollywood.*

Like Kubrick's previous films, *Paths of Glory* made no profit; however, it was praised by critics and became an influential anti-war film. Additionally, during the filming, Kubrick met a young German actress and artist named Christiane Harlan, who became Kubrick's third (and last) wife in 1959. Kubrick adopted Harlan's six-year-old daughter, and the couple had two more daughters, Anya Renata in April 1959 and Vivian Vanessa in August 1960.

Spartacus

Kubrick worked with Kirk Douglas for a second time in 1959 on Douglas's production of *Spartacus*, an epic tale set in ancient Rome. Douglas had fired the film's director in the first week of filming and asked Kubrick to finish the job. Kubrick accepted the offer and flew to Los Angeles with only three days' notice.

Kubrick's film Lolita *tells the story of a middle-aged man's sexual involvement with an adolescent girl. Although audiences and critics enjoyed the film, many religious groups condemned it.*

Directing *Spartacus* lasted for several months and was a difficult and unpleasant experience for Kubrick and for almost everyone else involved. The crew and cast did not know Kubrick and were not happy with his unusual methods and his aloof personality. Further, Kubrick and Douglas were both strong-willed men with large egos, and they clashed regularly over how to shoot the film.

Kubrick and the Censors

After *Spartacus*, Kubrick vowed to never again work for anyone else nor film in Hollywood. It was a vow he kept: For the remainder of his career, he filmed exclusively in the United Kingdom, since it gave tax breaks to foreign filmmakers as long as they hired 80 percent of the crew locally.

Kubrick's first film shot abroad was *Lolita*, based on the popular 1955 novel by Vladimir Nabokov. After the arduous, frustrating, and lengthy task of filming *Spartacus*, shooting *Lolita* was relatively easy. However, getting the film past the censors in England and America proved to be difficult because of the subject matter. In Nabokov's novel and the film, the protagonist, a middle-aged writer and teacher named Humbert Humbert, enters into a romantic and then sexual relationship with his landlady's adolescent daughter. Although the book and the film were satiric and tame by contemporary standards, at the time *Lolita* earned an X rating in England, meaning children under sixteen years old were not allowed admittance. Further, Kubrick had to make numerous edits in the film in order for the Motion Picture Association of America to approve it for release in the United States.

Despite the edits, the film was controversial upon release. Many groups, including the Catholic Church and the Legion of Decency, condemned it. However, audiences and critics enjoyed the film. It made over $4.5 million—about twice what it had cost, making it Harris-Kubrick's first profitable film. It was also the last film made by Harris-Kubrick. Harris wanted to direct his own films, so the two men parted amicably, remaining friends for the rest of Kubrick's life.

War Comedy

Kubrick's next film, on his own, *Dr. Strangelove*, was at least equally controversial as *Lolita* because its subject matter: nuclear war. Like many people during the Cold War, Kubrick was concerned about the possibility of nuclear war between the United

Actor Slim Pickens takes a break while filming Dr. Strangelove, *Kubrick's dark comedy about nuclear war.*

States and the Soviet Union. Kubrick channeled these concerns into his film, a black comedy set in a fictionalized near future in which a mentally deranged U.S. Army officer triggers a nuclear conflict with the Soviets without government authorization of his actions. As the film ends, possible full-scale nuclear destruction begins with the detonation of a hydrogen bomb.

Although the subject matter was risky and many warned Kubrick against making the film, he went through with it anyway for the sake of producing good art. Harris said, "Stanley believed that you shouldn't be inhibited by what people are going to think of you, whether they're going to like you or not . . . for you have to live with your work to the end of your life."[20]

As expected, when the film was released in 1964, many people attacked it as irresponsible, anti-American, and in bad taste. However, the positive reaction by many more critics as well as audiences was the best in Kubrick's career up to that time. The film also garnered Kubrick his first Academy Award—for best director—as well as the Writers Guild Award for best screenplay of 1964. With *Dr. Strangelove*, Kubrick achieved status as an international director and producer.

Into the Future

Soon after the release of *Dr. Strangelove*, Kubrick began working on a science fiction film, unaware at first that it would become the most ambitious and important project of his career. Science fiction became a popular movie genre in the 1950s; however, Kubrick considered most of the films to be artificial and cinematically primitive. He wanted to undertake a realistic as well as artistically sophisticated project.

To develop a story line, he hired science fiction writer Arthur C. Clarke to collaborate with him on a screenplay based on a few of Clarke's short stories. However, instead of a traditional screenplay, Clarke wrote the story as a novel to be used as a guide for further improvisation.

The story, titled *2001: A Space Odyssey*, begins at the dawn of humanity, at which time early Homo sapiens come in contact with a mysterious extraterrestrial monolith on Earth. Afterward, one of the early humans invents the first weapon—a club, which he and his tribe use to destroy another competing tribe. The story then jumps in time and location from 2 million years B.C. on Earth to the year 2001 in space near the Jupiter moon IO, where a space exploration crew has been mysteriously stranded after contact with a monolith identical to the one shown earlier in the film.

Kubrick used cutting-edge special effects and futuristic set designs during production of his science-fiction classic, 2001: A Space Odyssey.

While Clarke worked on the novel, Kubrick amassed a large science fiction library, hiring a staff to find and accumulate everything in print and on film so that he could study it. He was particularly interested in studying special effects in films, which he planned to use extensively for the first time in his career.

MGM financed the film's production, which eventually ran to $10.5 million, $6.5 million of which was for the special effects required to depict the exterior shots of space. These were all shot without the benefit of computer animation, which was not yet available, so instead the effects were done using models and other techniques. In all, the film contained 205 special effects, requiring sixteen thousand separate shots and over a year's time after the principal photography was finished.

The film was due in America in April 1968 for a press release. Kubrick brought the film from England on the *Queen Mary*, working up to the last minute in a special film editing room set up on the ship.

Recognition and Wealth

The public and critical reaction to *2001* was radically divided, largely along generational lines. Christiane Kubrick remembered, "If you were under thirty you dug the film, and if you were over thirty you came out of the cinema bored and perplexed in equal measure, generally speaking."[21]

Initial reviews and box office reports were disheartening, but over a period of weeks after its release, *2001* became increasingly popular among the baby boomers who were in their teens and twenties in 1968. Over time, the film proved to be one of the most profitable in cinema history. It was rereleased five times during the 1970s and made over $40 million, becoming one of MGM's five most successful films.

The special effects were revolutionary, inspiring a new era of special effects films, such as *Star Wars, Close Encounters of the Third Kind, Blade Runner*, and others. The film also influenced a new generation of science fiction directors, including James Cameron, and Steven Spielberg, who later wrote, "[*2001*] had tremendous influence over all my work and over my generation's race to space."[22]

The film also made Kubrick quite wealthy, ensuring that he would never have to work for anyone else. He and his family bought a large estate in Hertfordshire on the outskirts of England, where he and Christiane both set up workshops for their art projects. Some criticized him for leaving America, but he explained his move as a professional preference. He said,

> Because I direct films, I have to live in a major English-speaking production center. That narrows it down to three places: Los Angeles, New York, and London. I like New York, but it's inferior to London as a production center. Hollywood is best, but I don't like living there.[23]

Recluse

As he grew older, Kubrick left the estate less and less, and rarely traveled outside the United Kingdom, becoming a recluse who preferred to remain out of the public eye and spend his time in the company of a small number of colleagues, friends, and family members. He conducted most of his business by telephone and fax (and later by e-mail), colleagues came to the estate to meet with him and worked from there, and before the advent of videotape, he kept up on new films by having them brought to the estate for private screenings in his personal theater.

His absence from the public eye encouraged rumors about him to develop. Many characterized him as paranoid, excessively safety conscious, and even mentally deranged. However, the people who knew him say that he was simply protective of his privacy. As writer Michel Ciment said, "Although Kubrick was reclusive, he was certainly no hermit. It was his conscious choice, not some neurotic compulsion that led him to reject, early in his career, the endless obligations that accompany glory: travel and speeches, urbanity and self-aggrandizement."[24]

Controversy, Violence, and Art

Especially in his later career, Kubrick's films were the most visible thing about him, and his ninth film, *A Clockwork Orange*, was among his most visible because of the controversy it created. Kubrick adapted the screenplay from British novelist Anthony Burgess's satiric book by the same title. Like the book, the film portrayed a dystopic near future in which gangs of wanton youths

Kubrick's controversial film A Clockwork Orange *(pictured) initially received an X rating for its graphic depictions of violence and sexual assault.*

perpetrate brutal crimes for enjoyment. Alex, the protagonist played by actor Malcolm MacDowell, was the leader of one of the gangs and one of the culture's worst offenders.

The movie contained numerous acts of violence on screen, including assault, rape, and murder; in England and the United States the film was given an X rating because of the sexual content. The film was also denounced by the Catholic Church and many conservative religious groups in both countries. Many reviews reviled the film because of its subject matter, but many critics liked it. The film was nominated for three Oscars and was awarded the New York Film Critics prize for best film of the year, and Kubrick was awarded for best director of the year.

Unfortunately, outbreaks of copycat crimes allegedly inspired by the film broke out in England and the United States, including an attempted assassination of presidential candidate George Wallace. Many groups called for the film to be banned in England, where the crimes had been particularly prevalent. A pessimist about the condition of humanity, Kubrick defended the film, saying that violence was a natural state of man and integral to art. He said, "There has always been violence in art. There is violence in the Bible, violence in Homer, violence in Shakespeare, and many psychiatrists believe that it serves as a catharsis rather than a model."[25]

Even though he did not believe that A Clockwork Orange had been the cause of the violence, he pulled the film from circulation in England. Nevertheless, for years afterward Kubrick was personally harassed for making the film. His wife wrote, "We received hate mail and death threats."[26]

The threats continued into the production of his next movie, Barry Lyndon, in 1974. Originally shot in Ireland, the film was shut down and moved to England following reported death threats from the Irish Republican Army, a group with strong ties to the Catholic Church, which had denounced A Clockwork Orange and Kubrick personally.

Twenty Years, Three Films

The furor and threats over A Clockwork Orange only reinforced Kubrick's tendency to stay out of the public eye in the last twenty-five years of his life. Few pictures of him were available and he rarely gave interviews. So little was known about what he was doing that a New York con man named Alan Conway successfully passed himself off as Kubrick for several years in the 1990s. Until he was found out, Conway gave interviews and took advantage of the accolades and privileges the lie brought him.

Jack Nicholson appears in a terrifying scene from The Shining, *one of only three movies Kubrick made between 1975 and 1999.*

Additionally, from the mid-1970s to the late 1990s, Kubrick released only three films: *The Shining* in 1980, *Full Metal Jacket* in 1987, and *Eyes Wide Shut* in 1999. Despite the paltry number of films for the amount of time, Kubrick was rarely not thinking about or working on a film. However, as he explained, finding the appropriate subject often took a long time. He said, "The hardest thing for me is finding the story. . . . [I]t takes so long to find something worth doing."[27]

Last Years

In 1997, Kubrick completed filming *Eyes Wide Shut.* The film was a dark, dreamlike story about the marital discord between a couple, played by then-married actors Tom Cruise and Nicole Kidman. The film had taken fifteen months to shoot and Kubrick spent the last year of his life editing it, often working eighteen

Filmography of Stanley Kubrick

Eyes Wide Shut	(1999)
Full Metal Jacket	(1987)
Shining, The	(1980)
Barry Lyndon	(1975)
Clockwork Orange, A	(1971)
2001: A Space Odyssey	(1968)
Dr. Strangelove	
or: How I Learned to Stop Worrying and Love the Bomb	(1964)
Lolita	(1962)
Spartacus	(1960)
Paths of Glory	(1957)
Killing, The	(1956)
Killer's Kiss	(1955)
Fear and Desire	(1953)

hours a day to try to complete the film by a July 1999 release date. However, on March 7, 1999, he died unexpectedly in his sleep at age seventy-one.

Kubrick was buried in the garden on his England estate with a small funeral attended by family and a few friends, including Cruise and Kidman, directors Sydney Pollack, Mike Leigh, and Steven Spielberg, and his old friend and colleague James B. Harris.

Although Kubrick had completed the editing of *Eyes Wide Shut*, those who knew him said that he would have been tinkering with it until the last minute. He never saw the final version of the film. When it was released the film received mixed reviews. However, Kubrick was widely eulogized by critics, filmmakers, and others as a genius and one of the twentieth century's most important filmmakers. His films, particularly *Dr. Strangelove, 2001*, and *A Clockwork Orange*, remain some of the most influential and popular films, and numerous directors cite Kubrick's work as among the key influences in their careers.

CHAPTER 3

Francis Ford Coppola

Francis Ford Coppola became a filmmaking legend almost overnight in 1971 with his film *The Godfather*. Before and since that time, he struggled to achieve and maintain artistic integrity and creative independence in the face of disasters, including ruinous debt, bankruptcy, lawsuits, marital discord, and other troubles. These troubles often arose from Coppola's inclination toward risk and his stubborn refusal to let problems or doubts sway him from finishing even his most ill-advised projects. However, because of these characteristics, Coppola became renowned as one of America's boldest and most creative filmmakers.

Artistic Heritage

Coppola was born April 7, 1939, in Detroit, Michigan, the second of three children of second-generation Italian Americans Carmine and Italia Coppola. The couple's other two children were a son, Augustus, born in 1934, and a daughter, Talia, born in 1945.

Coppola's parents were a glamorous couple who were proud of their Italian culture. Carmine Coppola was a talented solo flutist who spent Coppola's entire childhood waiting for a never-arriving breakthrough in his career. Because of the nature of Carmine Coppola's job, the family moved frequently. According to Coppola, "It was in my father's gypsy nature not to stay in any one place too long."[28] The family moved from Michigan to New York when Coppola was young.

A Period of Isolation

Moving from place to place made it difficult for Coppola to make friends, and his isolation worsened when he contracted polio when he was nine. The disease caused him a great deal of pain and left the left half of his body paralyzed for a long time, during which he was forced to convalesce at home. Because of the highly contagious nature of the disease, he could not have visitors. Alone and confined to bed, Coppola was forced to entertain himself. He watched television, listened to records, and played with a 16 mm projector and tape recorder, developing an early love of machines

Filmmaker Francis Ford Coppola is pictured on the set of The Godfather III, *the final installment in the trilogy that brought the director lasting fame.*

and gadgets. Additionally, he made elaborate puppets to keep himself company and staged plays with them.

After a year of slow recovery and work with a physical therapist, he was able to leave the house. He later said that the period of illness and recovery was a growing experience. "I think any tough time you go through, any real crisis where you break down, then survive, leaves you in a far different place from where you were."[29]

An Evident Talent

As a result of spending so much time alone during his illness, when he returned to school, Coppola was an introvert and a self-described outsider. But he was a good student and a voracious reader with an active interest in science and a passion for writing.

After he graduated from high school in 1956, Coppola entered Hofstra University in New York. There he studied theater and developed an interest in filmmaking after seeing *Ten Days That Shook the World*, by Russian theater and film director Sergei Eisenstein. He said, "[After seeing the film] I was dying to make a film. So, following Eisenstein's example, I studied theater and worked very hard. . . . I wanted to . . . have the same breadth of knowledge as Eisenstein did."[30]

Coppola entered the drama department, where he crewed, building sets and operating the theater lighting, acted, and eventually wrote and directed plays for performance, becoming the most successful and well-known student in the department. When Coppola graduated from Hofstra University in 1960, he enrolled in film school at the University of California, Los Angeles (UCLA).

Making a Start

At the time, film schools were a new phenomenon, and Coppola thought there was too much talk and too little hands-on filmmaking involved. Impatient and driven, Coppola borrowed equipment and started making short films on his own. On the strength of his short work, a group of investors hired him to write a screenplay for a low-budget sex-themed film. Called *Tonight for Sure*, the film was released in 1961 and did well enough that he was asked to direct another similar film, called *The Playgirls and the Bellboy*, released the following year.

Working with Corman

Because of the subject matter of his first features, the work did not win Coppola much respect among his UCLA peers. However, Roger Corman, a well-known producer-director who specialized in cheap horror films, heard about Coppola and hired him as editor, screenwriter, script doctor, and fill-in director. Coppola loved the job and tried to impress his new mentor with his hard work. He recalled, "I'd deliberately work all night so when [Corman] arrived in the morning, he'd see me slumped over the [film editing machine]. He started to see me as an all-purpose guy."[31]

Coppola was hired to write the screenplay for the 1961 low-budget sex-themed film Tonight for Sure *(pictured).*

From Corman, Coppola learned a lot about low-budget film-making. For instance, when Corman finished filming one movie, he would quickly make another using the same cast and sets to double his productivity. On one such occasion, Corman let his protégé shoot his own horror film, *Dementia 13*, from a script Coppola had written. Corman liked the film enough to assign him another horror film, *The Terror*, starring then unknown actor Jack Nicholson.

Neither film did well critically or commercially when released, but Coppola did not care. He was working as a professional director and that was enough. Additionally, during the *Dementia* shoot, Coppola met and became romantically involved with a student named Eleanor Nell. The two married on February 2, 1963.

Moving Out on His Own

After two years with Corman, Coppola left to go out on his own. In 1963, Seven Arts Studios offered him $450 a week to work as a screenwriter for the company. Coppola accepted the offer and withdrew from UCLA.

The salary from Seven Arts allowed Coppola enough financial security to buy an expensive new car and a house for his new family, which included his and Eleanor's first child, a son, Gian-Carlo, born September 17, 1963. The new wealth also emboldened Coppola to risk the family's savings of $20,000 on the stock market. He hoped the profit would be enough to produce his first independent feature film, but unfortunately, the stock crashed and he lost every cent of the investment.

Despite the setback, he still had the steady income from his job. However, that soon changed. During an assignment working on a script in Europe, Coppola worked on his own project during off-hours, adapting a screenplay from the novel *You're a Big Boy Now*, for which he had purchased the rights. When he returned to the United States, Coppola asked Seven Arts to produce the film; however, the studio claimed that since Coppola wrote the script while under their employment, it belonged to them. After an argument, Coppola left Seven Arts, with the ownership of the script still disputed by both parties.

Coppola wrote the script for You're a Big Boy Now *(pictured) during his employment with Seven Arts Studios. As a result, the studio claimed ownership of the script.*

Money soon became a concern. He had a mortgage and bills to pay, as well as a growing family to support, including a second son, Roman, born on April 17, 1966. He took the first good job offered to him, which was to adapt the biography of World War II–era general George S. Patton into a screenplay for Twentieth Century Fox. The script was well liked, but the film was shelved and not released until 1970. Nevertheless, Coppola was paid for the job and used the money to start production on *You're a Big Boy Now*, after negotiating a contract with Seven Arts, who still claimed ownership of the script.

When the film was released in New York on March 21, 1967, it received mixed reviews and mediocre box office receipts; however, to Coppola it was a significant achievement since it was the first time he had put an entire film together himself, including the funding. As a last gesture to UCLA, he submitted the film to the college as his master's degree thesis. It was unprecedented for a film school graduate to have a nationally released film as a thesis, and the school granted the degree on the film's merit.

Role Model

Following the release of *Big Boy*, Coppola was offered numerous studio jobs; however, determined to remain independent, he declined all of them. He disliked the studio system, believing that the focus on box office returns stifled creativity because studios were afraid of risk and innovation. Working independently was a gamble, but he felt he had to take the chance while he was young. He said, "If I don't have the guts to do it now, I might never have the guts to do it ever."[32]

His next picture was a musical set in the 1940s called *Finian's Rainbow*. During filming, Coppola met a young film student from Modesto, California, named George Lucas. Lucas had wanted to work with Coppola because he respected him. Lucas recalled,

> I was in admiration of him because he was the first film student to break into the film industry. At that point, film students just didn't make it into the film industry. You had to be related to somebody or know somebody; the idea that you could get there with an education and knowledge and skill and talent was unheard of. Francis was the first one to break through, so all of us students were very much in awe of him.[33]

Coppola and Lucas became friends, and Lucas also worked on Coppola's next film, *The Rain People*, a low-budget road movie filmed on location in several locations across the country.

Coppola directs Fred Astaire during the filming of Finian's Rainbow. *Although the film was a commercial failure, Coppola was determined to remain independent.*

American Zoetrope

When released, both *Finian's Rainbow* and *The Rain People* flopped at the box office. Nevertheless, Coppola was determined to remain independent. With Lucas and two other filmmakers, Ron Colby and Mona Skager, Coppola opened his own film studio in a warehouse in San Francisco, California. The studio was called American Zoetrope, and Coppola envisioned it as an untraditional repertory company and a new direction in filmmaking. According to the studio, "[Coppola] decided he would build a deviant studio that would conceive and implement creative, unconventional approaches to filmmaking."[34]

Coppola struck a deal with Warner Brothers–Seven Arts for a loan of $300,000 against the success of the company's first two pictures. According to the deal, if the pictures were not profitable, Coppola would be responsible for repaying the loan. This put the studio at considerable financial risk. Coppola later admitted that the deal was a mistake but that he lacked business experience. "My enthusiasm and my imagination far outpaced any kind of financial logic,"[35] he said.

The studio's first film was *THX 1138*, written and directed by Lucas. When the Warner Brothers–Seven Arts executives saw the film on November 19, 1970, they hated it and called off their deal with the studio. American Zoetrope was forced to close soon afterward.

The Godfather

After the closing of American Zoetrope, Coppola became desperate for work. Then Paramount Pictures studio executive Robert Evans approached him to write and direct a film based on the best-selling Mafia crime novel *The Godfather* by Mario Puzo. *The Godfather* follows the story of New York's leading Mafia family during the 1940s and 1950s as it struggles to maintain control of its crime organization. Coppola at first turned down the offer. He wanted to remain independent and did not want to make a film about the Mafia, believing its reputation promoted negative stereotypes about Italian Americans. However, Coppola's financial situation was dire enough that he finally accepted the job.

Actors Marlon Brando (right) and Al Pacino perform a scene from The Godfather. *Coppola initially rejected the offer to write and direct the famous Mafia drama.*

Making *The Godfather* was extremely difficult and trying for Coppola. From the beginning, Evans and Coppola disagreed over almost every aspect of making the film. Further, many in the cast and crew had little confidence in Coppola. He later admitted that some of their doubts were well founded, as he had never shot a film of the scope and expense of *The Godfather*.

The mood on the set was so serious and tense that Coppola more than once considered quitting; however, during the filming his ego and credibility received a much-needed boost when he won his first Academy Award for Best Adapted Screenplay for *Patton*, which Coppola had written for Twentieth Century Fox in the late sixties and which had finally been released.

Further, when *The Godfather* was released in March 1972, it was an astounding success, breaking records for attendance and box office sales. Audiences responded well to all of the elements of the film, including the script, the direction, the performances, and the score. Additionally, many enjoyed the vicarious thrill of living in the Mafia where honor, loyalty, and family were juxtaposed with extortion, revenge, and murder. The film also did well critically, garnering Golden Globe awards and a Directors Guild Award for Coppola. Additionally, Coppola received a percentage of the box office receipts, and the success of the film made him a millionaire.

Wealth and Independence

Suddenly wealthy beyond his dreams, Coppola purchased a mansion in San Francisco and a historic estate with a vineyard in Napa, where he eventually established a winery. Professionally, the money gave him freedom and independence to do what he wanted. Paramount offered him a chance to do a sequel to *The Godfather*, but he declined. Instead he directed an opera for the San Francisco Opera, became the owner-publisher of San Francisco–based *City* magazine, opened a theater and acting school, produced George Lucas's second film, *American Graffiti*, and wrote a screenplay adaptation of F. Scott Fitzgerald's novel *The Great Gatsby*, which was directed by Jack Clayton.

Then, in 1974, Coppola directed and produced *The Conversation* from a script he had written a few years before to produce through the American Zoetrope studios. Although the studios had closed, Coppola reopened American Zoetrope's business and production offices in San Francisco's North Beach area. He then produced the film conjointly with The Directors Company, formed the same year by Coppola, Paramount Pictures, and filmmakers Peter Bogdanovich and William Friedkin.

Reviewers in Europe loved *The Conversation*, but it received mixed reviews in the States and earned less money than it cost to make. Nonetheless, the film earned Coppola the prestigious Golden Palm for Best Film at the Cannes Film Festival. Further, the film eventually became a classic thriller, ranking among Coppola's most popular films.

The Godfather: Part II

Despite Coppola's commitment to remaining independent from the Hollywood studio system, in 1973 Paramount lured him with a $1 million fee to write and direct a sequel to *The Godfather*. *The Godfather: Part II* posed its own challenges and troubles, but unlike his state of mind during the first film, Coppola was more confident in his abilities and was able to bring the project in on time and within budget. While the film was not equal to its predecessor in box office success, it was even more well received critically, winning numerous awards, including six Academy Awards for Best Screenplay, Best Director, Best Picture, Best Art Direction, Best Supporting Actor (Robert De Niro playing a young Vito Corleone), and Best Musical Score, the latter going to Nino Rota and Coppola's father, Carmine Coppola.

Into the Jungle

After *The Godfather: Part II*, Coppola returned to his independent projects, the next being a film about the Vietnam War that had been in the back of his mind for several years. Eventually titled *Apocalypse Now*, the idea for the film was developed by screenwriter John Milius and George Lucas in the late 1960s. The plot was based on English novelist Joseph Conrad's novella *Heart of Darkness*, set against the backdrop of the war in Southeast Asia.

As written, the film was not intended as an antiwar statement but as an examination of the dark side of human nature; however, because the film negatively portrayed the military and the war, the U.S. Department of Defense refused to provide any technical assistance or cooperate with Coppola on the project.

This was only one of the first of many difficulties that slowed and burdened almost every phase of the project throughout its production. Casting, financing, and finding a location to shoot took months longer than it should have.

Coppola handled the difficulties as best he could; however, he spent much of his time distraught, believing that the film would be a disaster. He was also worried about financial ruin. Within a few weeks of the beginning of the shoot, he had already gone over

Dennis Hopper (left) and Martin Sheen (second from left) appear in a scene from Coppola's Apocalypse Now. *Filming in Southeast Asia complicated production of the film.*

budget and had to take a loan of $3 million from United Artists, for which he would be personally responsible if the film did not make $40 million in box office receipts.

The stress of the shooting conditions was exacerbated by excessive drug use by cast and crew alike during the filming. Coppola admits that he smoked too many cigarettes, and, for the first time in his life, smoked marijuana. His personal life also experienced significant strain as his marriage began to fall apart, in part because he was involved in an extramarital affair, which he eventually ended.

In May 1977, at the end of the shoot, which had taken 238 days at a cost of $27 million, almost everyone involved felt as though the film had been their own private war. In fact, Coppola later said, "The way we made it was very much like the way the Americans were in Vietnam. We were in the jungle, there were too many of us, we had access to too much money, too much equipment, and little by little we went insane."[36]

The End of the Journey

After nearly two years of postproduction work, which required Coppola to edit over a million feet of footage, the film premiered in August 1979. Although critics found much to praise about the first two-thirds of the film, most found the last third a confusing mess. The confusing ending occurred, in part, because Coppola himself had not known how to conclude the film until near the end of the shoot. One reviewer called the film "a failed quest—in common modern form—a search for the holy grail that doesn't exist."[37]

In 1979, after nearly three years of filming and postproduction work, Coppola released Apocalypse Now *to mixed reviews from critics and audiences.*

New Technologies

The difficulties of location shooting in *Apocalypse Now* convinced Coppola to make his next film as much as possible in a studio where he could control conditions. In 1979, he acquired the historic 1920s Jasper Hollywood Studio in Los Angeles to create Zoetrope Studios. There he began producing pictures for other filmmakers while taking a rest and looking for the right story for his next project.

Meanwhile, Coppola explored the advances being made in new electronic cinema technologies such as videotape recording, which promised to cut costs and save time. Using these technologies, Coppola developed a lengthy previsualization process that involved, among many other steps, shooting an entire film on video before committing any images to celluloid film. Further, during shooting he used regular movie cameras in tandem with video recorders, which allowed him to play back shots immediately. The traditional process of rush-developed "dailies" required several hours between shooting and playback.

Risking It All

Coppola employed the new electronic cinema technology for the first time on a fablelike love story that takes place in Las Vegas, Nevada, called *One from the Heart*. Additionally, Coppola made the unusual choice to shoot the entire film in the studio, spending millions to re-create Vegas streets and interiors on a set. These innovations excited Coppola. He told the press, "On one level, *One from the Heart* is a thrust into a new technology. . . . It's different from anything I've done before—anything anyone's done before."[38]

Unfortunately, as well planned and useful as the technological innovations were, they added so much cost to the preproduction that the savings benefit that might have been gained in shooting or postproduction was eliminated. Because of the technologies and the choice to film in the studio, the budget ballooned from $15 million to over $23 million. During the weeks of shooting, the film was constantly under threat of being shut down because of lack of money, and Coppola had to raise $8 million by taking out personal loans, using his studio, his house, and other properties as collateral. By the end of the project, he was so financially indebted that he risked losing almost everything he owned if the film was a failure.

Which it was. In fact, *One from the Heart* was one of the biggest flops of Coppola's career. Many reviews were so bad that they bordered on hostility toward Coppola. Further, the film made only about $800,000 in the first twenty days of release, forcing Coppola to take the film out of circulation before it had run a month.

Horribly in debt and faced with bankruptcy of his studios and the possibility of even losing his home, Coppola was forced to put Zoetrope Studios up for sale less than two years after it opened. Coppola left for Tulsa, Oklahoma, in part to hide from the disappointment, the ringing telephone, and financial woes while he made a small film called *The Outsiders*.

Refuge in Tulsa

The Outsiders had been an extremely popular novel for young adults written by S.E. Hinton. Coppola adapted the screenplay and in the spring of 1981 went into preproduction, making the picture through Zoetrope Studios before the sale of the studio was final.

Coppola enjoyed making the film a great deal. The cast was filled with young actors, most of them little known, but who would go on to successful careers. Among them were Tom Cruise, Rob Lowe, Diane Lane, and Matt Dillon. The actors gave Coppola much needed respect and admiration, and the shoot of the film went smoothly. Coppola recalled that the film helped alleviate his problems back in Los Angeles: "It turned into a way for me to soothe my heartache over the terrible rejection [of *One from the Heart*]."[39]

Recalling his days with Roger Corman, before leaving Tulsa Coppola decided to make a second film to double his productivity there. He used several members of *The Outsiders* cast and shot *Rumble Fish*, another film based on an S.E. Hinton novel. *The Outsiders* was commercially successful, making in its first weekend more than five times what *One from the Heart* had made during its entire run; however, *Rumble Fish* did so poorly that it was pulled from circulation a few weeks after its release.

A Period of Trials and Tragedy

The rest of the 1980s was a difficult time for Coppola. The failure of *One from the Heart* had diminished his reputation to the point where he had to work as a director for hire rather than on his own projects. The films he made between 1983 and 1989 were critically and commercially mediocre. They included *The Cotton Club*, a large-scale film about the jazz era in Harlem; *Peggy Sue Got Married*, a time-travel romantic comedy starring Kathleen Turner and Coppola's nephew Nicholas Cage; *Gardens of Stone*,

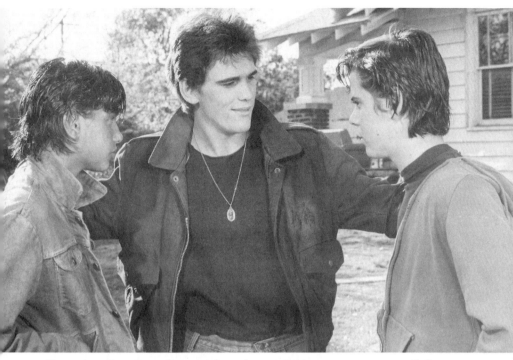

Coppola enjoyed working with such promising young actors as (left to right) Ralph Macchio, Matt Dillon, and C. Thomas Howell on the set of The Outsiders.

Coppola's second Vietnam film; and *Tucker: The Man and His Dream*, about an independent automaker. He also made two short films: *Captain EO* for Disney theme parks and *Life Without Zoe*, for a film anthology of shorts called *New York Stories*.

During this professionally difficult period for Coppola, personal tragedy struck his family on Memorial Day weekend in 1984 when their eldest son, Gian-Carlo, who had left school at sixteen to work with his father in the movies, was killed in a boating accident during a filming break of *Gardens of Stone*. Coppola was devastated. "He was a magical kid . . ." he said. "There's always going to be something missing [from my life]. It'll never come back, I guess."[40]

The Godfather, Again

By the late 1980s, Coppola was struggling to regain the creative control and freedom he had known in the 1970s following *The Godfather*. He wanted to reestablish his Zoetrope Studios and work on his own films again. However, in 1989, he was enticed by Paramount to make a third *Godfather* film, *The Godfather:*

Part III. Recalling the popularity of the first two films, Coppola believed the sequel might make it possible for him to go back to his independent work.

Coppola accepted the job and worked hard to keep the project on schedule and budget. However, the film was not as profitable as Coppola had hoped, and it failed to make enough money to rescue him from his financial difficulties. It would take a fifteenth-century vampire to revive Coppola's finances from the dead.

Dracula

While filming *The Godfather: Part III*, Coppola agreed to direct *Dracula*, a film adaptation of the nineteenth-century novel by Irish writer Bram Stoker. While the novel had inspired dozens of films since the first adaptation, *Nosferatu*, in 1922, few of the adaptations had followed the 1897 novel very closely. However, the script for this version, written by James V. Hart, focused on the real-life fifteenth-century warrior figure, Vlad Tepes, upon whom Stoker based the character of Dracula. Coppola helped revise the script over the summer of 1991 and began shooting the film later that year.

Coppola earned $5 million for directing the film, in addition to about 10 percent of the gross. With his director's fee, he was able

Coppola's 1991 version of Bram Stoker's Dracula *(pictured) was a commercial success and allowed the director to return to independent filmmaking.*

Filmography of Francis Ford Coppola

Rainmaker, The	(1997)
Jack	(1996)
Dracula	(1992)
Godfather: Part III, The	(1990)
Tucker: The Man and His Dream	(1988)
Gardens of Stone (as Francis Coppola)	(1987)
Peggy Sue Got Married (as Francis Coppola)	(1986)
Cotton Club, The (as Francis Coppola)	(1984)
Rumble Fish	(1983)
Outsiders, The (as Francis Coppola)	(1983)
One from the Heart	(1982)
Apocalypse Now (as Francis Coppola)	(1979)
Godfather: Part II, The	(1974)
Conversation, The	(1974)
Godfather, The	(1972)
Rain People, The	(1969)
Finian's Rainbow	(1968)
You're a Big Boy Now	(1967)
Terror, The (uncredited)	(1963)
Dementia 13 (as Francis Coppola)	(1963)
Playgirls and the Bellboy, The	(1962)
Tonight for Sure	(1961)

to settle some debts and purchase additional real estate, including a mountain lodge and adjoining jungle property in Belize. He planned to restore the lodge as a family vacation property if *Dracula* was successful.

When released in November of that year, the film was a resounding commercial success, making over $54 million in ten days. Coppola's financial worries were finally behind him. For the first time in years, he was totally debt free.

With the pressure relieved, he was able to again focus on making the films he wanted to. He told the press that he had had enough of the Hollywood film industry and that he was not cut out for it. He said, "I need to be a solo guy. . . . I'm just not going to participate [in the Hollywood system] any more. I'm going to experiment with my own ideas—experiment without fear that failure will finish me off."[41]

Recent Years

As of 2004, Coppola had directed only two other films, the Robin Williams comedy *Jack* in 1996 and the adaptation of John Grisham's legal thriller, *The Rainmaker*, in 1997. However, Coppola was closely involved in filmmaking in other capacities. Since 1990, he produced or executive produced over forty films, including his daughter Sofia Coppola's films *The Virgin Suicides* and *Lost in Translation*.

Coppola's love of technology has never waned. Through American Zoetrope he helped pioneer several technological advances in the industry, including digital sound and editing processes. In addition to its filmmaking activities, the company also produces a literary magazine called *Zoetrope All-Story* and in 2004 ran its second annual screenplay writing contest. Coppola always saw himself as a screenwriter first, emphasizing the all-important script as the foundation for any film.

Further, Coppola's Niebaum-Coppola estate winery in Napa has for almost two decades produced wine from its vineyards. After the winery became increasingly successful during the 1990s, Coppola branched out into the restaurant and resort businesses, opening the Café Niebaum-Coppola in San Francisco and Palo Alto and resort properties in Belize.

Legacy

Critics have said that Coppola's career peaked early and that his most important work has been behind him for decades. Even Coppola admitted that his work during the 1980s and 1990s was not as critically substantial as his work in the 1970s. However, throughout his career Coppola remained an important figure, a director with whom most actors wanted to work and whose artistic abilities have rarely been doubted. In addition to his personal projects, particularly *The Conversation* and *Apocalypse Now*, his *Godfather* films have become influential classics. Coppola also helped to create Don Vito Corleone, whom *Premiere Magazine* rated first in a list of one hundred all-time favorite film characters. Moreover, Coppola led the way for a generation of film school–graduate directors and championed new ideas and means in independent filmmaking.

CHAPTER 4

Spike Lee

Spike Lee's career is among the most successful of his generation. To date, he has directed thirty-one film and television projects, produced or executive produced thirty-one, written thirteen screenplays, appeared in eleven films, and written several books, including a children's book coauthored with his wife, Tanya Lewis. He is also a sought-after lecturer, is the owner of several profitable companies, has served as an assistant professor at Harvard University, and has appeared in numerous commercials.

Additionally, since the late 1980s, Lee has remained unchallenged as the most influential and successful African American director in the country. This fact is made more remarkable given that he has spent his entire career purposely shocking and provoking audiences and critics, often making them uncomfortable and angry while entertaining them at the same time. Indeed, many critics contend that this is Lee's gift and purpose—to be the entertaining troublemaker, to confront people with serious issues while engrossing them in the stories he tells. In doing so, he has made history. No black director before him gained the accolades, financing, and power within the entertainment industry, and those who came after owe at least some portion of their success to him.

Heritage

Spike Lee was born Shelton Jackson Lee on March 20, 1957, in Atlanta, Georgia, the first of five children of William "Bill" Lee and Jacqueline Shelton Lee. His younger siblings were brothers Chris and David, born in 1958 and 1960, respectively, a sister, Joie, born in 1963, and a brother, Cinqué, born in 1968. Jacqueline Lee gave Shelton the nickname "Spike" when he was still an infant. He later said, "She said I was a tough baby. The nickname stuck."[42]

Bill Lee was a jazz musician who played the upright bass, backing such famous musicians as Billie Holiday, Duke Ellington, and Chick Corea; Jacqueline Lee was a teacher who encouraged her children to take pride in their heritage. The Lee family had a rich history, which could be traced back six generations to two

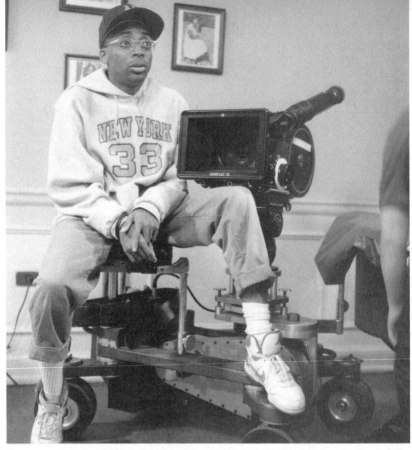

Since the 1980s, Spike Lee has been the most successful African American filmmaker. His films combine entertaining storytelling with thought-provoking subject matter.

Africans who had been kidnapped by slave traders and sold into slavery in America. Given the slave names Mike and Phoebe, they were then split apart, but only temporarily, as Lee recounted. He recalls, "Mike worked three or four years to buy his freedom and walked from South Carolina to Alabama to reunite with his wife and family. I'm a descendant of him. That's my family. We've always been very strong, very proud, fearless, and intelligent."[43]

Lee's more immediate heritage was equally impressive. His great-grandfather, William James Edwards, studied at the Tuskegee Institute, founded by Booker T. Washington, and became an educator, author, and founder of one of the oldest black colleges in America, the Snow Hill Institute in Snow Hill, Alabama. His father and mother were also well educated, his father having attended Morehouse College in Atlanta and his mother having attended Spelman College, Morehouse's sister school. The two met during college and married after graduation to start their family.

A Culturally Rich Childhood

Lee's parents influenced their children in different ways. His father was a relaxed parent. Lee says, "My father had expectations for us, but his way was the hands off, natural way. His philosophy was, let them do whatever they want and somehow they'll do the right thing. So my mother had to be the bad cop, the enforcer."[44]

Jacqueline pushed her children to excel in school and get good grades. She also introduced them to literature, art, and film; meanwhile, Bill Lee often allowed Spike to come along with him on gigs to watch him play. He said that this cultural influence affected all the kids in the family. "For me it's no accident that a lot of my siblings and myself are artists. . . . You know, it comes from exposure, if you're exposed to art at a very young age, [you will likely become an artist]."[45]

Lee was also influenced early on by his surroundings. When he was a toddler, his parents moved the family to New York so Bill Lee could get more steady work. They moved to the borough of Brooklyn, into the Cobble Hill neighborhood, where they were

Growing up in Brooklyn had a profound influence on Lee. He used the borough as the setting for some of his films, including Do the Right Thing *(pictured).*

the only black family in the then predominantly working-class Jewish, Italian, and Puerto Rican area. While Lee remembers being called names a few times because he was black, he soon fit in well, playing sports with the other neighborhood kids. From an early age, he was a natural leader and a strong athlete. He recalled that his first dreams were of becoming a professional athlete, never realizing that he would become a filmaker:

> Growing up I wanted to be an athlete. The sport didn't matter; it just depended on what season it was: basketball, football, baseball, I played 'em all and still love 'em today. I had no idea that people made movies. I just didn't know. You went to the movie house, the lights went out, the movie came on, you enjoyed it . . . the lights came on, and took your ass home. Movies were magic—and something you couldn't do. Or so you thought.[46]

Education

Lee's parents provided the family with a middle-class existence, and they were eventually able to buy their own home, a brownstone in the predominantly working-class neighborhood of Fort Green. However, Bill Lee often had trouble finding work because he was a jazz purist, only willing to play the upright bass rather than the electric bass, which was popular in rock. Because of this preference, money was frequently scarce. Lee remembers his family eating dinner by candlelight many evenings when the electricity had been turned off. His father's behavior also taught him a lesson that would influence his own career. He recalled,

> My father was never really a business man. And I'd have to say he really helped me by not being one. What I mean by that is I understood from being my father's son that talent alone is not nearly enough. My father has always been a greatly talented musician, but it takes more than that [to succeed]. You've got to have business sense, too.[47]

Lee graduated from high school in 1975 and moved back to Atlanta to attend his father's alma mater, Morehouse College. He lived with his maternal grandmother, Zimmie Shelton, who had saved money for years to pay her grandchildren's college tuition. Lee's grandmother's support meant a great deal to him and drove him to succeed. "She always had complete faith in me,"[48] he said.

Lee loved Morehouse and loved being in Atlanta where most of the accomplished people around him were black. "It was just a

Lee shows his support for the basketball team of his alma mater Morehouse College in Atlanta, Georgia, where Lee first began making films.

great feeling to be in an environment in which all your classmates and all your teachers were African Americans,"[49] he said.

Although he was not a top student, he was actively involved in extracurricular activities. He worked on the college newspaper and hosted a jazz program on the student radio station. He also organized the college's first intramural softball team.

Tragedy struck while Lee was in his second year at Morehouse. His mother died of cancer, leaving his father alone to care for his younger siblings. Lee decided to stay at Morehouse to finish his education. That same year, while studying for his mass communications major, he began filmmaking for the first time.

The Summer of '77

When Lee returned to New York for summer break in 1977, he purchased a Super 8 (8 mm) movie camera and began shooting film on the streets. That summer turned out to be highly eventful. It was one of the hottest summers on record, and a large blackout resulted from the drain on the electrical grid caused by the excessive use of cooling systems. During the blackout, massive looting and violence occurred, and Lee shot a lot of footage of it. The summer of 1977 in New York was also the height of the disco dance craze called the Hustle. Lee filmed people dancing and then combined the footage with what he had captured during the

At New York University, Lee made a number of short films that dealt with race issues. Lee created a revised version of the racist film Birth of a Nation *(pictured) early on.*

blackout to create his first film, a documentary called *The Last Hustle in Brooklyn*, which he submitted as part of his degree.

By the time Lee graduated from Morehouse in 1979, he knew he wanted to be a filmmaker but felt that he did not yet have the necessary skills. He took an internship at Columbia Pictures during the summer and then returned to New York in the fall to start a three-year degree program at New York University's (NYU) prestigious film school.

Stirring Up Trouble

At the time he entered NYU, Lee was one of very few blacks in the program. He quickly made a reputation for himself by making controversial short films that dealt with race issues. For example, his first short told the story of a black screenwriter rewriting the infamous D.W. Griffith film classic, *Birth of a Nation*, which depicted the early Ku Klux Klan in a heroic light.

In his second year, he was given a teaching assistantship that paid his tuition and allowed him to use the money his grandmother gave him to produce films. Although Lee enjoyed shocking his fellow students and professors, he wanted to make commercially successful films. He wanted to explore the black experience in America but also to entertain people. He said, "I did not want to have my films shown only during Black History Month in February or at libraries. I wanted them to have wide distribution."[50]

To that end, in his last year at NYU, he made a short comedy called *Joe's Bed-Stuy Barbershop: We Cut Heads*, about a fictional African American–run barbershop in Brooklyn that fronted for a gambling ring. The film was financed by his grandmother, the music was scored by his father, and his friends and family members worked as cast and crew. The film ended up winning a Student Academy Award as well as the prestigious New Director's/ New Films Series Award.

Making It on His Own

With this illustrious close to his film school career, Lee thought he would get immediate work but instead ran into his first experience with the white-dominated film industry. He remembered,

> Being young and dumb and naïve, I thought because of this award that all the studios would call me up and within a year I would be directing films in Hollywood. That was not the reality. I finished school in 1982, and the climate for African-American directors was not the same as today. . . . Back when I began, you had to be Michael Shultz, the only African-American director working, and Eddie Murphy and Richard Pryor. They were there, but that was about it."[51]

Lee realized that he had to make his own opportunities, which meant making his own films. He took a job working in the shipping department of First Run Features, a small independent distribution company. In the meantime, he worked on a script called *The Messenger*, about a bicycle messenger in New York. He borrowed money from friends and family and began preproduction on the film; however, because it was to be filmed entirely on location, expenses ran high and he ran out of money before he was able to even begin shooting. The dilemma was agonizing as he worried over his failure and the loss of money to his investors. Finally he had to cancel the project.

She's Gotta Have It

With his lesson learned about the expense and difficulty of filming on location, Lee wrote another screenplay called *She's Gotta Have It*, which was set entirely in a single apartment and in a park near where he lived. Despite his previous failure, he was able to borrow funds. He also won an $18,000 grant from the New York State Council on the Arts to add to the budget. However, he ran out of money again quickly, so he and his cast and crew wrote letters to everyone they knew asking for contributions. The film took twelve days to shoot, with cast and crew working almost around the clock and Lee doing everything. He recalled, "We were shooting sixteen, seventeen hours a day. . . . You know, it was do or die. I had no money at all, but . . . I had to worry about everything, including the costumes."[52]

The final cost ended up being $175,000, which Lee was barely able to cover with the contributions sent in. However, Island Pictures agreed to distribute the film, and on its release in 1986, it earned Lee the much-coveted young filmmakers' Prix de Jeunesse Award at the Cannes Film Festival. It also was enormously successful commercially. While some thought the film would have limited appeal because of its predominantly black cast, it drew audiences of all colors and made $8 million, a huge profit.

Outspoken Celebrity

The critical and commercial success of his debut feature film made Lee an overnight celebrity, a status of which he took full advantage. He appeared on magazine covers, talk shows, and commercials for Nike. He also used his new celebrity to voice his already outspoken opinions. He criticized comedienne/actress Whoopi Goldberg for wearing blue contact lenses and Michael Jackson for his numerous plastic surgeries, claiming they were denying their race and trying to look white. Further, he criticized director Steven Spielberg for directing *The Color Purple*, a film adapted from black novelist Alice Walker's book, claiming that a white director had no business making the film.

Early Controversy

The success of *She's Gotta Have It* gave Lee something he valued even more than celebrity: the financial ability to make his second feature film, *School Daze*. *School Daze* was a musical set on the campus of an all-black college, and it dealt thematically with how superficial differences among blacks, such as hair styles or the

Lee (right) performs in a scene from School Daze, *a controversial film that angered many prominent African Americans.*

lightness or darkness of skin color, divide African Americans from one another. Lee explains why he wrote the script. "I think one of the biggest misconceptions white America has about African-Americans is that we're a monolithic group. That we all think alike, dress alike, live alike."[53]

The subject matter made the film controversial even while it was in production, as many blacks accused Lee of revealing unflattering aspects of black culture. Even his alma mater, Morehouse College, where he began filming *School Daze*, threw Lee and his crew off campus when they learned what the film was about. Lee was unfazed and finished the production at Atlanta University; however, the controversy continued upon its release. Lee received harsh criticism about the film from blacks and black organizations, including the United Negro College Fund and television talk show host Bryant Gumbel, who hostilely attacked both the film and Lee.

Despite the negative press, the film made an $8 million profit. From the experience Lee learned that controversy over his films was in itself good advertising.

Race and Violence

Lee's third feature was his most controversial to date. Called *Do the Right Thing* and set in the racially diverse Bedford-Stuyvesant neighborhood of Brooklyn, the film dealt directly with prejudice and bigotry among the races. During the course of the film, which takes place over a twenty-four-hour period during a summer heat wave, the interactions among white Italian Americans, African Americans, and Asian Americans grow strained and eventually violent, resulting in the death of a black man and the arson of an Italian American–owned pizza parlor.

Before the film was released, some critics worried that the film would spark riots. Two white critics went on the *Oprah Winfrey Show* before the premiere to speak out against the film and discourage people from attending. Lee scoffed at the notion. He said, "I don't think that blacks are going to see this film and just go out in the streets and start rioting. I mean, black people don't need this movie to riot."[54] Although many whites did stay away from the theaters, opting to see it later on video, the film did very well critically and commercially. It won the praise of several critics as one

Lee's third feature-length film, Do the Right Thing *(pictured), dealt candidly with racial prejudice and bigotry in the United States.*

among the ten best films of 1989 and garnered the nomination for Best Original Screenplay at the Academy Awards, a first for an African American.

After the controversy over *Do the Right Thing*, Lee backed away from direct racial issues to make *Mo' Better Blues*, a tribute to jazz, his father's great passion. However, his fifth film, *Jungle Fever*, a story about an interracial relationship between a black man and a white woman, was a return to race issues as well as the issue of drug abuse. Lee explained that drug use was an important issue to him for different reasons. He said,

> The story of drugs in that film was partially personal. My father, a jazz musician, had been involved in heroin. But even more important than that, my number one priority . . . was knowing how crack is destroying the African-American family in this country. For me that was the heart of the story.[55]

However, it was the race issue that was most discussed by critics. Many accused Lee of being prejudiced against interracial relationships because the protagonists in the film finally are unable to make their relationship work. But Lee corrected the critics. "We're not trying to condemn interracial relationships," he said. "People have to realize that this film does not represent every single interracial couple in the world."[56]

Malcolm X

Lee's next film was to be his most ambitious to date and would become a landmark of his career. Lee heard that Warner Brothers was beginning preproduction on a film based on *The Autobiography of Malcolm X*, the true-life story of a former street criminal who joined the Nation of Islam while in prison and became its most prominent minister after his release. Malcolm X became a powerful and well-known leader in the American Muslim community during the 1960s, at the height of the civil rights movement. However, in 1964, after a pilgrimage to Mecca, which changed his views on the relationship of race and the Muslim religion, he left the church, alienating Nation of Islam leader Elijah Muhammad and angering many Muslims. Malcolm X was assassinated in February 1965 by members of the Nation of Islam; however, he remained a powerful inspiration to many involved in the civil rights movement and today still remains one of the most important, as well as one of the most controversial, figures in American history, particularly among blacks.

Actors Denzel Washington (right) and Angela Bassett are featured in Malcolm X. *Lee suffered several financial setbacks while making the film.*

The project proved to be a great challenge. Since the late 1960s, many filmmakers had attempted to make a film on Malcolm X's life, but none had succeeded. Lee explained that in part the difficulty was the challenge of showing him as both a man and a public figure. "Malcolm meant so much to so many people," he said. "He has achieved sainthood. . . . My challenge was to show his greatness and his humanity. . . . We didn't want him to be some mythic, god-like, Christ-like figure who was above everybody else."[57]

Further, practical problems arose, such as budgetary constraints on the film. Warner Brothers would fund the film for only $26 million when the budget required at least $33 million. However, Lee decided the film was too important to delay. He said, "If we didn't try to do this right now at this moment, it might be another twenty more years. So we took the leap."[58]

Almost predictably, critics began speaking out about the film before it was done. Many, such as poet Amiri Baraka, expressed concern over how Lee would portray Malcolm X, afraid Lee would focus more on the figure's early criminal years rather than his latter years of leadership and service. Another prominent critic of the film was Malcolm X's widow, Betty Shabazz, to whom Lee had shown the screenplay. She hated it, claiming it misrepresented the couple's marriage.

Troubles On and Off the Set

Further, the filming was fraught with disasters both personal and professional. During the shoot, Lee's girlfriend broke up with him and his father was arrested for heroin possession. Also, one of the extra actors on the film was found murdered in her apartment. These events made headlines in the media for weeks as the tabloids exploited the drama.

The largest professional difficulty during the filming was that Lee ran out of money. By the end of the shoot, the film had gone way over budget. However, as he had done during the filming of his first feature, Lee used his imagination to raise funds to keep the production alive. He wrote to prominent black entertainers and figures for financial investment, receiving money from celebrities including Tracy Chapman, Bill Cosby, Janet Jackson, Michael Jordan, and Oprah Winfrey to finish the film. Additionally, he convinced Warner Brothers to come up with extra funding for the increasingly anticipated and controversial film.

Upon its release, the critics were surprised at how uncontroversial the film was. Many were disappointed because the film failed to live up to the buildup and hype that had preceded its release. Actor Denzel Washington, who played Malcolm X, received much

Washington received an Academy Award nomination for his stirring performance as the militant African American leader Malcolm X.

attention and praise for his performance, including an Oscar nomination for Best Actor; however, at $48 million, the film was not the commercial success Warner Brothers had hoped it would be.

Malcolm X, however, was the biggest-budget black-directed film in history, and Lee was very proud of it. He considered the film the best thing he had done. Additionally, the scope of the *Malcolm X* project proved that Lee, still in his early thirties, was the top African American director in the country.

Life Away from the Camera

Life away from the camera had also become increasingly rewarding for Lee. While his personal life had been something he tried to keep out of the media, many speculated about his romantic life. He had been linked with model Veronica Webb and actress Halle Berry in the past, but in 1993, he married attorney Tanya Lewis. Lee described his wife as intelligent and his closest confidante and adviser. He said,

> She's the first one who reads, as soon as I finish a script. Whenever I'm thinking about doing something, she's the first one I tell. Everybody has peers and people they respect. You have to listen to those people, not to the hype and not to the people who just don't know.[59]

Later in 1993, the couple had their first child. Still an avid sports fan, Lee named her Satchel after legendary black baseball player Satchel Paige. The couple's second child, a son, born in 1997, was named Jackson after Reggie Jackson, another renowned black baseball player.

Additionally, Lee received prestigious professional accolades away from the camera. In 1992 he was made a visiting professor at Harvard University. Additionally, he accepted a position on the board of Morehouse College.

A Rigorous Decade

Lee kept up a rigorous filmmaking schedule throughout the 1990s, making six features, two documentaries for film, and five for television. While none of the work released in the 1990s was received with as much controversy or attention as his earlier work, he continued to work to call attention to issues of race. His 1996 documentary *4 Little Girls* recalled the bombing by racists of an African American church in Birmingham, Alabama, during the civil rights movement, an incident that took the lives of four young girls. The following year, his feature *Get on the Bus* dra-

Lee's 1999 film Summer of Sam *(pictured) upset many critics for its portrayal of serial killer David Berkowitz, who referred to himself as the Son of Sam.*

matically portrayed the stories of several men traveling across the country to attend the One Million Man March on Washington D.C., which took place in October 1996. This film was funded entirely by contributions by participants in the real-life march.

Perhaps the most controversial of his films during the 1990s was *Summer of Sam*, released in 1999, which was set in New York City during the summer of 1977—the events of which had served as documentary material for his first film, *Last Hustle in Brooklyn*. The controversy arose over the portrayal of the serial killer David Berkowitz, who called himself the Son of Sam and terrorized areas of the city with a string of random murders. Many critics objected to the movie's inclusion of the serial killer; however, Lee explained that the film was not about Berkowitz but about how the violence and tensions of that summer changed the lives of so many people.

In addition to fifteen film and television projects he completed in the 1990s, Lee also started various business ventures, including

Filmography of Spike Lee

She Hate Me	(2004)
25th Hour	(2002)
Bamboozled	(2000)
Summer of Sam	(1999)
He Got Game	(1998)
4 Little Girls	(1997)
Get on the Bus	(1996)
Girl 6	(1996)
Clockers	(1995)
Crooklyn	(1994)
Malcolm X	(1992)
Jungle Fever	(1991)
Mo' Better Blues	(1990)
Do the Right Thing	(1989)
School Daze	(1988)
She's Gotta Have It	(1986)
Joe's Bed-Stuy Barbershop: We Cut Heads	(1983)

a production company, a music company, an advertising agency, and a store of Lee-related merchandise called Spike's Joint in Brooklyn. Further, he made numerous commercials for corporate sponsors such as Nike, Levis, and Diet Coke. While some accused Lee of selling out, he defended his business endeavors:

> I am a capitalist. We all are over here. And I'm just trying to get the power to do what I have to do. To get that power you have to accumulate some type of bank. And that's what I've done. I've always tried to be in an entre-preneurial mode of thinking. Ownership is what's needed amongst Afro-Americans. Ownership. Own stuff.[60]

Continuing the Fight

In recent years Lee has remained active in film and television. Released in 2000, *Bamboozled* was among his most confrontational features yet. In it, a frustrated black television producer proposes a television version of a blackface minstrel show.

Since 2000, Lee has made two other features and several documentaries, and is at work on a series for the Showtime cable station called *S.F.C. (Sucker Free City)*. The plot of *S.F.C.* will revolve around the conflicts among white, black, Latino, and Asian street gangs in San Francisco. Thus, race will continue to be a focus of

Lee's work, as it has been since the beginning of his career. While he acknowledges that racism will not be eradicated by his work, he sees it as his mission to bring it into the open. "I think the best thing my films can do is provoke discussion," he said. "In my films, I try to show that there's a very serious problem."[61]

Lee's plans for the future are much as they were when his career began: to keep working hard. "I expect to be doing this until I die," he said. "[Although] I'm not going to be making a film a year when I'm 80. . . . It's not just about quantity, it's about creating a body of work that will stand the test of time."[62]

Lee's body of work continues to evolve and remain strong and innovative. Additionally, in spite of his relatively young age given his accomplishments, Lee has already created a legacy, making it easier for black artists to break into filmmaking. He has also set an example for artists of all races who want to challenge the status quo in society and film.

CHAPTER 5

Peter Jackson

Few viewers in America knew who Peter Jackson was before his incredibly successful series of *The Lord of the Rings* films. The New Zealander was considered a Hollywood outsider who had made films only in his native country, which had almost no notable film industry prior to Jackson's career.

A completely self-taught filmmaker, Jackson built upon his early blood-and-gore "splatter films" to create increasingly ambitious and critically acclaimed work until he grabbed the attention of Hollywood in the mid-1990s with the thriller *Heavenly Creatures*. Soon, Jackson became a much sought-after filmmaker in America; however, unlike many foreign directors acclaimed in the States, Jackson remained in New Zealand where he used his new wealth and reputation to create his own community of independent companies. This community provided him with everything but the financing required to make films, including the elaborate and spectacular special effects that have become his signature.

Only in his early forties when his third *The Lord of the Rings* film swept the Oscars in 2004, Jackson established himself as a film legend. He also brought his home country's film industry into the limelight for the first time.

Boyhood in Pukerua Bay

Peter Jackson was born on October 31, 1961, in Wellington, New Zealand, the only child of Bill Jackson and Joan Ruck, who had emigrated separately from England in the 1950s because of the poor economic conditions in the United Kingdom following World War II. "They were very working class," said Jackson, "They both left [England] within a year or two of each other and they met here in New Zealand."[63] The couple married in Wellington and settled in the nearby coastal town of Pukerua Bay, where they took jobs with the city.

Pukerua Bay had a population of only about eight hundred people, and, raised there as an only child, Jackson spent much of his early childhood finding ways to entertain himself. He explored the outdoors a great deal. The family's house had a garden that ran to

Early in his career, New Zealand–born filmmaker Peter Jackson built a reputation as a director of graphic blood-and-gore films.

the edge of a steep cliff that dropped a thousand feet to the sea, and the terrain all around was dramatic and magical to Jackson. "There were lots of hills and forests and gullies and caves,"[64] he recalled.

Jackson also spent a good deal of time building model airplanes and watching movies and television. He was obsessed about movies, particularly the 1932 version of *King Kong*, which he watched repeatedly, marveling at the stop-action special effects by which the filmmakers animated the colossal ape. He recalled, "I knew *King Kong* wasn't real when I saw it. . . . I still loved it even after I could see in the fur the thumbprint of the man who moved the armatures on the model."[65] He also admired British comedy shows, particularly *Monty Python's Flying Circus* because "[the troupe] took intellectual concepts and then applied them to silly things,"[66] he said later.

He loved film so much that his parents, who supported their son's artistic flair, bought a Super 8 movie camera for him as a Christmas gift when he was eight years old. Jackson spent hours making films alone and with friends from school. In some, he

As a child, Jackson was fascinated with the stop-action special effects of the 1932 version of King Kong.

imitated the stop-action technique used in *King Kong* to animate models and toys, and he and his friends re-created entire *Monty Python* skits for the camera. He also created some of his first special effects, filming model planes caught on fire and creating World War II battles, simulating gunfire by punching holes in the film. His first completed short film, made in 1971 when he was ten, cost him twelve dollars, all of which he made back by charging neighborhood children and classmates admission to watch.

In making his early films, he developed a love not only for special effects but also for telling stories, the latter being a by-product of the former. He said, "I realized through my own kind of filmmaking process that the real fun was in the storytelling. I'd be trying to invent little stories so that I could show off my models."[67]

Weekend Filmmaker

By the time Jackson became a teenager, he had already acquired considerable skill in making films. In 1978, he entered a television contest with an eighteen-minute short film, *The Valley*, which garnered him a cash prize. He also became a cineast, developing admiration for directors such as Stanley Kubrick, Martin Scorsese, and Buster Keaton.

When he graduated from high school in 1979, he already knew he wanted to be a filmmaker and applied for a job at a postproduction filmmaking laboratory called Film Unit, one of the few movie-related businesses in the region. He was turned down for the job, so he took a job as a photoengraver with Wellington Newspapers, Ltd., preparing photos for publication in the *Evening Post*.

While working, he persisted with his filmmaking, making movies on weekends. He started a feature-length vampire film called *Curse of the Gravewalker* in 1981 but later abandoned the project. Then, in 1983, his father gave him another movie camera, this one a 16 mm Bolex, with which he set to work on what would become his first complete feature, *Bad Taste*.

Bad Taste started as a short test film with the new camera. Originally called *Roast of the Day*, the story of the film—planned around the special effects he created, like his earlier work—was a strange mixture of plots involving zombielike creatures, aliens, and cannibals, and many of the film effects involved splattering blood and gore. The theme and effects revealed the influence of recent zombie and gory horror films. Jackson said that he was inspired by "that five- or six-year stretch [in the late 1970s to mid-1980s] when George Romero was [making *Dawn of the Dead*],

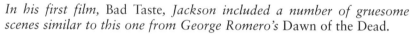

In his first film, Bad Taste, *Jackson included a number of gruesome scenes similar to this one from George Romero's* Dawn of the Dead.

Sam Raimi was making his 'Evil Dead' films and Stuart Gordon was making 'The Reanimator.'"[68]

Working for years on weekends and holidays with a crew and cast of fellow photoengravers from work, Jackson added to the film as he developed more effects. Jackson also acted in the film, playing two characters because "I ran out of friends,"[69] he said. News about Jackson's film got around to other creative people in the area, including a young woman named Frances Walsh, who came to assist with the film. Walsh was an aspiring screenwriter who offered to help work on the script; however, Jackson admitted that no script had ever been written for the film. He set her to work painting sets instead. Jackson later said that before he met Walsh, "I didn't know any girls at the time. I was a geek."[70] Walsh and Jackson became friends and then romantically involved, marrying in 1987. The two also developed a long-standing professional partnership with Walsh working on every film Jackson made.

In addition to time and friends, the film required money, so in 1985 Jackson wrote a letter to the New Zealand Film Commission (NZFC) for a grant. After viewing the raw footage of the film, most of the commission's members were not enthusiastic; however, Jim Booth, the chair of the commission, thought the film had a lot of promise and pushed for Jackson to receive a grant to finish the film. They awarded Jackson $128,000 in installments of $5,000, beginning in 1986. Jackson later reflected with mischievous pleasure at the award:

> The subversive streak in me gets an incredible kick that somehow in my career I essentially got the New Zealand government, through the film commission, to finance these incredibly gory films. I'm sure they're the only government in the world that's ever financed splatter films.[71]

Launching His Career

The film was finished in 1987, and after four years of work on the film, with the support of the NZFC, Jackson entered *Bad Taste* at the Cannes Film Festival in May. The critics loved the film, and distributors from thirty countries bought the rights to it. Within a few days of its first showing, the film had more than paid for itself. In the summer of 1987 it premiered in Wellington to good audience response. Even the critics seemed to get the film's humor. One wrote, "*Bad Taste* . . . is a clumsy, cheap, and often hilarious shotgun wedding between alien-takeover film and cannibal farce."[72]

The success of *Bad Taste* at Cannes allowed Jackson to quit his job as a photoengraver to become a full-time filmmaker. In 1988, Jim Booth quit the NZFC and joined Jackson to form a film production company, WingNut Films. The first project they intended to make was a zombie film, and Jackson and Booth met with foreign investors to gather enough money to produce it. However, the funds fell short of what the film would require, so Jackson postponed the movie and began work on another project called *Meet the Feebles*. The script for *Meet the Feebles* was written by Jackson, Walsh, and friends Danny Mulheron and Stephen Sinclair. The film was a bizarre puppet show story with characters including a hippo and her philandering walrus husband, as well as a cast of costar puppets dealing with a host of adult-themed problems such as blackmail, drugs, and AIDS.

The project, first developed by Mulheron, had been in Jackson's mind for a few years, and he had even filmed a short version of it while working on *Bad Taste*. From April through July 1989, he filmed the full-length version in Wellington in a railroad shed near the Parliament Building. When it was premiered in Italy in October, it did well. People appreciated the bizarre humor, one critic calling it "*The Muppet Show* on Acid."[73]

Following the release of *Meet the Feebles*, Jackson and Mulheron were commissioned by New Line Cinema to write a script for the next *Nightmare on Elm Street*, a popular horror film series. The two finished the script in early 1990, but in the meantime New Line had purchased another script.

Zombies!

Although he was disappointed in the missed opportunity with New Line, upon its New Zealand release *Meet the Feebles* made enough money for WingNut Films to allow Jackson to do the zombie movie he had put on hold. With Walsh, Sinclair, and Mulheron, Jackson rewrote the early version of their script and began filming in late 1991 at Avalon Studios in Wellington and on location around the city. The film, which would eventually be called *Braindead*, was the largest and most expensive film he had done yet, as well as a first working with professionals. "I directed actors for the first time," he recalled, "So it was like a real movie."[74]

Braindead premiered at Cannes in May 1992 and was very popular. It was then released in the United States in February 1993 under the title *Dead/Alive*, and there it received even greater critical acclaim and commercial success than his other films. Jackson was interviewed by numerous people and for the first time became

Jackson's 1992 zombie film Braindead *received critical acclaim at the Cannes Film Festival, giving Jackson his first taste of celebrity stardom.*

a celebrity. Not used to the attention, Jackson remained modest about his work. "I was just a guy who loved zombie films and badly, badly wanted to make a zombie film," he said.[75]

Thanks to the success of the U.S. release of *Dead/Alive*, Jackson's first two features, *Bad Taste* and *Meet the Feebles*, were rereleased on a larger scale. The three films together gave Jackson a solid reputation as a "splatter film" director. However, Jackson was not happy with the characterization. He said, "I was perceived as being a splatter director, which is fine. I mean, I'm proud of my splatter movies. . . . But it is interesting that that somehow automatically makes [people think you are] incapable of directing anything else."[76]

Changing His Image

Jackson's next project would challenge critics' narrow perception of his abilities. He and Walsh spent several months working on a screenplay based on the true story of a 1954 murder committed by New Zealanders Pauline Parker and Juliet Hulme, two teenage girls whose obsessive and intimate relationship with each other led them to murder Parker's mother. Jackson described how the project began:

Fran [his wife] had been really interested [in the case] when she was a kid. Fran [wanted] to find out who these girls were—what journey they went on that ended in them killing one of their mothers. We loved the script process because we had to behave like investigative journalists. Everything in the movie was taken from people's memories.[77]

Jackson and Walsh interviewed approximately forty people, including seventeen of the girls' classmates. They found it difficult to get information from people, however, because "New Zealand is a very closed off society," said Jackson. "We don't celebrate our famous murders the way America does. We tend to shut the door and pretend it never happened."[78] Nonetheless, through much work the couple was able to get enough material for their screenplay for the film, called *Heavenly Creatures*. Jackson shot the film over three and a half months in and around the town of Christchurch, where the murders had occurred.

The postproduction of *Heavenly Creatures* was a lengthy process that required numerous special effects shots to bring to life the elaborate fantasy world that the two protagonists of the film created in their imaginations during their relationship. To allow him the independence to work in New Zealand on the special effects, Jackson formed his own special effects company, WETA Limited.

Jackson, his film crew, and the actors prepare to shoot a scene for the 1994 film Heavenly Creatures.

He also purchased the already established Camperdown Studios in Wellington to allow him the ability to do more studio work.

The postproduction lasted well into 1994, during which time Jackson's WingNut partner, Jim Booth, died of cancer. Jackson mourned the loss of his partner, with whom he had made his first three films.

Heavenly Creatures premiered in July 1994 in Wellington. The American studio Miramax was impressed by the film and signed Jackson to a deal whereby Miramax would have first chance to produce his next films in return for purchasing the majority of the international rights to *Heavenly Creatures*. In February 1995, the film was released in the United States to such success that *Bad Taste* and *Meet the Feebles* were released in the United States for the first time.

At that time, *Heavenly Creatures* was Jackson's most critically acclaimed film. In September 1994, it won the prestigious Silver Lion Prize at the Venice Film Festival. It also garnered an Academy Award nomination for Best Original Screenplay for Jackson and Walsh. However, Quentin Tarantino's script for *Pulp Fiction* won instead.

Branching Out

Jackson's film success allowed him to branch out into producing other films and to do some work for television. He executive produced a film by New Zealand director Tony Hiles called *Jack Brown Genius*, the script for which was written by Hiles, Jackson, and Walsh. Then in April 1995, Jackson and his friend Costa Botes, a writer for the *Ray Bradbury Theater* television series, made a mock documentary for New Zealand television in which they created a heroic New Zealand filmmaker named Colin McKenzie.

Meanwhile, Jackson's film *Heavenly Creatures* had become a significant critical and commercial success in America, where it caught the attention of director Robert Zemeckis, who, like Jackson, had made his reputation in part as a great special effects director with films such as *Back to the Future* and *Who Framed Roger Rabbit?* Zemeckis contacted Jackson and asked him and Walsh to write a script for an episode of the TV series *Tales from the Crypt*, which Zemeckis planned to direct.

A Halloween Film in the Summer

Jackson and Walsh spent a few weeks on the script, a comedic horror story that Jackson described as "*Casper* meets *Silence of the Lambs*"[79] and delivered it to Zemeckis, who liked it so much

Michael J. Fox (center) stars in The Frighteners. *Jackson and Frances Walsh originally submitted the story as an episode of the TV series* Tales from the Crypt.

he said it was too good for the low-budget television film he had originally planned. Instead, he suggested that Jackson direct the film and he would executive produce it. Jackson agreed and began filming in May 1995 at his studio in Wellington and in Lyttleton.

The film, called *The Frighteners*, starred Michael J. Fox as a con man who uses psychic abilities acquired as a result of a car accident to enlist ghosts to help him make money with fake exorcisms. He then gets mixed up in a series of mysterious murders for which he becomes the prime suspect.

Filming finished in November 1995, but postproduction took the rest of the year and early 1996 because 573 special effects had to be added to the film, which Jackson's company, WETA Limited, produced.

The Frighteners was a crowd-pleasing film, but it garnered neither the commercial nor the critical success of *Heavenly Creatures*. Nonetheless, Jackson was proud of it. And Universal and Miramax agreed to sign Jackson to a two-picture deal.

Staying in New Zealand

Particularly because of his last two pictures and now the deal with two major Hollywood studios, Jackson was asked whether he would move to America to make his films. He said that although making films in New Zealand was more difficult, he would not relocate. "Dealing with Hollywood on a regular basis would drive me crazy,"[80] he said.

Indeed, Jackson continued to create a small moviemaking empire in his native country. In December 1998, he purchased the postproduction company Film Unit—the same company that had denied him a job when he was seventeen—because it was on the verge of going out of business. He saw the necessity of acquiring it to save it. "New Zealand was about to face having no lab to process film and nowhere to do sound for post-production. We'd have to go to Australia to do it. So I had no choice, as someone who wants to base himself here, to buy that lab."[81]

The purchase was good timing for Jackson. In 1997 he embarked on a new film project that would require all of his professional and creative resources for the next several years of his life.

Despite offers to move, Jackson continues to make films in his native New Zealand instead of relocating to work in Hollywood.

From Ghosts to Hobbits

In 1995, soon after signing the deal with Universal and Miramax, Jackson asked Miramax chief Harvey Weinstein to look into who owned the rights to *The Hobbit* and *The Lord of the Rings* fantasy adventure novels written by British novelist J.R.R. Tolkien in the late 1940s and early 1950s. The books, which became popular for the first time in the 1960s, are set in the mythical land of Middle Earth, populated by elves, dwarves, wizards, and small human-like creatures called hobbits. *The Hobbit* tells the story of a hobbit named Bilbo Baggins, who embarks on a quest for treasure; *The Lord of the Rings* is the story of two hobbits, Frodo and Sam, who undertake a dangerous quest to save Middle Earth.

Although the rights to *The Hobbit* were unavailable at the time, Jackson was able to acquire the rights to *The Lord of the Rings*. In 1997, Miramax agreed to produce an adaptation of the novel, which Jackson and Walsh would write. Jackson and Walsh were surprised at the deal because even with Jackson's success with *Heavenly Creatures* and *The Frighteners*, he was not a sure bet or a well-known director for a project that would require a large budget and a long period of time to shoot. "We knew it was impossible," he later said, "[but] the fact that it happened doesn't make it any less impossible."[82]

Jackson and Walsh originally developed the script as a two-film installment. However, in July 1998, Miramax pulled out of the deal because they were willing to risk financing on only one film, not two. They gave Jackson four weeks to find another studio to finance the film. Fortunately, he was able to negotiate a deal with New Line Cinema for a three-picture rendition of *The Lord of the Rings* for $180 million. New Line founder Robert K. Shayne said that despite the poor record for sequels, he was willing to take a "leap of faith"[83] on the film because Jackson planned to shoot the principal photography for all three films at once, which would alleviate the difficulties that plagued many sequels, such as reassembling a cast of busy professional actors. "Could it backfire? Sure, if the first film is a disaster," he said. "But . . . we feel very certain that [*The Lord of the Rings*] has a universal currency in terms of interest."[84]

Ups and Downs

The Lord of the Rings was an enormous creative and professional undertaking for Jackson. The project would take over seven years of his life to complete, during which time he would also experience some significant changes in his personal life. In 1997 and 1998, Walsh and Jackson had two children, Billy and Katie, who spent all of their early childhoods watching their parents work on the film. Jackson said, "Lord of the Rings is all they've really known in their lives. . . . They've grown up with their mummy and daddy making [it]."[85]

Additionally, Jackson suffered the loss of both of his parents during the project. He later recalled how important their support had been to his life as a filmmaker:

> My dad died before we started shooting, and then Mum died about four or five days before we finished the first film. She never saw it. She was trying to hang on but she couldn't. I was only able to become a filmmaker because I had the support of my parents. I think if you're a kid who wants to make models and get a movie camera for his birthday, to become a filmmaker seems like a dream. I think parents have a choice if they have a child who dreams of an impossible career, of something that sounds crazy. My parents did everything they possibly could to make it happen for me.[86]

The filming began in October 1999 and lasted until December 2000, during which Jackson and his cast and crew worked long days with few breaks. The shoot was hard on him, and he frequently lost confidence in the film as it went along. This adversity prompted him to work harder on it. He said, "When you realize that every day you spend on a movie it will get better, it becomes difficult to take a day off."[87] From the beginning, Jackson spent a great deal of energy imagining how to shoot the film and how to incorporate the special effects to create a believable world. "We wanted to make this world real and allow you to enter it," he said. "The trick is to say, 'This isn't fake; it happened. But it was six or seven thousand years ago. There were elves or trolls and they aren't around anymore but they used to be here and the records have been lost.' That's helped people engage with the film."[88]

Record Breakers

After a year of postproduction on the first part of the trilogy, *The Fellowship of the Ring* was released worldwide in eighteen countries in February 2002. Whatever doubts Jackson had about the film were alleviated by the response. The film broke box office records, making $860 million, $313 million in the United States alone. It was nominated for thirteen Oscars and won four: Best Cinematography, Best Visual Effects, Best Makeup, and Best Score.

Cate Blanchett and Elijah Wood perform a scene from The Lord of the Rings: The Fellowship of the Ring. The Lord of the Rings *trilogy has proved a monumental success for Jackson.*

It also ranked among the nine most-nominated films in Academy Award history.

Commenting on the success, Jackson attributed it to having enough time to do a proper job on the film. "Movies today are put through the factory system and rushed and then within 12 weeks they're in theaters. Bang! Shoot it and get it out there. . . . The trick is we had three years of preproduction on this . . . before the first day of photography and then it was 15 or 16 months of filming. Each film has a year of post-production [to do]. Hardly any film (today) has that."[89]

The second installment, *The Two Towers*, was released in December 2002 and was even more successful commercially than the first, making over $922 million globally; however, it was less critically acclaimed, being nominated for only six Oscars and winning two, for Best Sound Editing and Best Visual Effects.

The third film in the trilogy, *The Return of the King*, was by far the most successful of the three. Released in February 2003, it grossed over $1 billion worldwide and in 2004 made Academy Award history by winning each of its eleven nominations, including Best Picture. Only two other films in history—*Ben Hur* and *Titanic*—had won as many. It also garnered Jackson his first Academy Award for Best Director.

Jackson admitted that although awards do not enter his thinking while making a movie, acclaim is hard to ignore:

> It's not something that is really even part of the filmmaking process. You go on set, you write them, you shoot and edit them and you're simply focused on trying to make the most entertaining film you can. . . . I'm not part of the industry that makes films [in Hollywood]. I'm not on the social circuit. [But] it's not something you dismiss; it's not something you can say, "I don't really care."[90]

Jackson poses with his wife, Frances Walsh, after The Return of the King, *the third film in* The Lord of the Rings *trilogy, won eleven Academy Awards in 2004.*

Filmography of Peter Jackson

Lord of the Rings: The Return of the King, The	(2003)
Lord of the Rings: The Two Towers, The	(2002)
Lord of the Rings: The Fellowship of the Ring, The	(2001)
Frighteners, The	(1996)
Forgotten Silver	(1995)
Heavenly Creatures	(1994)
Braindead (Dead/Alive)	(1992)
Meet the Feebles	(1989)
Bad Taste	(1987)

The Future

The Lord of the Rings trilogy was a significant if not exhausting accomplishment, professionally and personally for Jackson. While in the process, he said that he wanted to make a smaller film after working with such an epic project. He wanted to return to New Zealand after the touring for *The Lord of the Rings* to make a New Zealand–based film. "New Zealand has tremendous stories. We have got quite a few ideas for New Zealand films," he said. However, in March 2003, Universal offered Jackson a chance to direct a remake of *King Kong*. Jackson could not refuse the project, he said. "I've wanted to remake King Kong since I was nine years old. I've got a cardboard model of the Empire State Building and a decomposing rubber King Kong mask that I made when I was nine or ten. . . . I'm pinching myself. . . . I agreed to do it without reading a script."[91]

Although *King Kong* was remade in 1976 and set in contemporary New York, Jackson plans to set his version in 1933, as the original was. Like *The Lord of the Rings* trilogy, Jackson planned to make the film primarily in New Zealand. He steadfastly declares that he wants to remain in New Zealand:

> I regard myself as a New Zealand–based filmmaker, and every time I've made a movie . . . I've seemed to use [the country] somehow to enhance my little filmmaking infrastructure here. . . . I've sort of been building a mini-[George] Lucas-type situation here, where I've ended up owning a postproduction facility, a studio, a film lab, a visual effects company, a digital effects company. I'm going to always need to finance my films outside of New Zealand because there's no source of film financing here.

But even if I shot on location in another country, I'd tend to be one of those filmmakers who'd want to shoot the studio stuff down here and bring the post-production [work] back here.[92]

Regardless of where he works, however, Jackson's career for the first time put New Zealand on the filmmaking map. He is regarded by many as a hero in his home country, especially in his hometown of Pukerua Bay. Despite his fame and fortune, he remains modest and expresses some disbelief at the direction his career has taken. "I always thought I'd be doing low-budget, New Zealand Film Commission–financed movies," he said. "And I just find myself in a place now that I could've never dreamt. I consider myself to be extremely lucky."[93]

NOTES

Chapter 1: Alfred Hitchcock

1. John Russell Taylor, *Hitch: The Life and Times of Alfred Hitchcock*. London: Faber and Faber, 1978, p. 19.

2. Alfred Hitchcock, "The Woman Who Knows Too Much," in *Hitchcock on Hitchcock: Selected Writings and Interviews*, edited by Sidney Gottlieb. Berkeley: University of California Press, 1995, p. 51.

3. Hitchcock, "The Woman Who Knows Too Much," p. 51.

4. Alfred Hitchcock, "Life Among the Stars," in *Hitchcock on Hitchcock*, p. 28.

5. Quoted in Patrick McGilligan, *Alfred Hitchcock: A Life in Darkness and Light*. New York: Regan, 2003, p. 85.

6. Quoted in Taylor, *Hitch*, p. 81.

7. Alfred Hitchcock, "My Screen Memories," in *Hitchcock on Hitchcock*, p. 14.

8. Quoted in Gene Adair, *Alfred Hitchcock: Filming Our Fears*. New York: Oxford University Press, 2003, p. 45.

9. Quoted in McGilligan, *Alfred Hitchcock*, p. 164.

10. Steven Jay Schneider, ed., *1001 Movies You Must See Before You Die*. London: Quintet, 2003, p. 386.

11. Quoted in John Russell Taylor, "Surviving," in *Hitchcock on Hitchcock*, p. 59.

Chapter 2: Stanley Kubrick

12 Quoted in John Baxter, *Stanley Kubrick: A Biography*. New York: Carroll & Graf, 1997, p. 23.

13. Quoted in Norman Kagan, *The Cinema of Stanley Kubrick*. New York: Holt, Rinehart and Winston, 1972, p. 2.

14. Quoted in Vincent LoBrutto, *Stanley Kubrick: A Biography*. New York: Donald I. Fine, 1997, p. 34.

15. Quoted in Paul Duncan, *Stanley Kubrick: His Complete Films*. Koln, Germany: Tachen, 2003, p. 23.

16. Quoted in Baxter, *Stanley Kubrick*, p. 47.

17. Quoted in Kagan, *The Cinema of Stanley Kubrick*, p. 17.

18. Quoted in LoBrutto, *Stanley Kubrick*, p. 93.

19. Quoted in Duncan, *Stanley Kubrick*, p. 37.

20. Quoted in Michel Ciment, *Kubrick: The Definitive Edition*. New York: Faber and Faber, 2001, p. 202.

21. Quoted in Christiane Kubrick, *Stanley Kubrick: A Life in Pictures*. Boston: Bulfinch, 2002, p. 129.

22. Quoted in Kubrick, *Stanley Kubrick*, p. 9.

23. Quoted in Tim Cahill, "Stanley Kubrick" (interview), *Rolling Stone*, August 27, 1987, p. 37.

24. Quoted in Ciment, *Kubrick*, p. 305.

25. Gene Phillips, ed., *Stanley Kubrick: Interviews*. Jackson: University of Mississippi Press, 2001, p. 209.

26. Quoted in Kubrick, *Stanley Kubrick*, p. 139.

27. Quoted in Ciment: *Kubrick*, p. 243.

Chapter 3: Francis Ford Coppola

28. Quoted in Peter Travers, ed., *The Rolling Stone Film Reader: The Best Film Writing from* Rolling Stone *Magazine*. New York: Pocket, 1996, p. 377.

29. Quoted in Michael Schumacher, *Francis Ford Coppola: A Filmmaker's Life*. New York: Crown, 1999, p. 10.

30. Quoted in Harlan Lebo, *The Godfather Legacy*. New York: Fireside, 1997, p. 16.

31. Quoted in Jeffrey Chown, *Hollywood Auteur: Francis Coppola*. New York: Praeger, 1988, p. 19.

32. Quoted in Schumacher, *Francis Ford Coppola*, p. 52.

33. Quoted in Schumacher, *Francis Ford Coppola*, p. 58.

34. Quoted in American Zoetrope, www.zoetrope.com.

35. Quoted in Lebo, *The Godfather Legacy*, p. 22.

36. Quoted in Chown, *Hollywood Auteur*, p. 126.

37. Quoted in Jon Lewis, *Whom God Wishes to Destroy: Francis Coppola and the New Hollywood*. Durham, NC: Duke University Press, 1995, p. 48.

38. Quoted in Lewis, *Whom God Wishes to Destroy*, p. 54.

39. Quoted in Schumacher, *Francis Ford Coppola*, p. 316.

40. Quoted in Travers, *The Rolling Stone Film Reader*, p. 381.

41. Quoted in Lewis, *Whom God Wishes to Destroy*, p. 162.

Chapter 4: Spike Lee

42. Quoted in Robert J. Emery, *The Directors: Take One.* New York: TV, 1999, p. 142.

43. Quoted in K. Maurice Jones, *Spike Lee and the African American Filmmakers: A Choice of Colors.* Brookfield, CT: Millbrook, 1996, p. 75.

44. Quoted in Caroline V. Clarke, *Take a Lesson: Today's Black Achievers on How They Made It and What They Learned Along the Way.* New York: John Wiley & Sons, 2001, p. 106.

45. Quoted in David Breskin, *Inner Views: Filmmakers in Conversation.* New York: Da Capo, 1997, p. 153.

46. Quoted in Spike Lee, Terry McMillan, and David Lee, *Five for Five: The Films of Spike Lee.* New York: Stewart, Tabori & Chang, 1991, p. 12.

47. Quoted in Spike Lee, with Ralph Wiley, *By Any Means Necessary: The Trials and Tribulations of the Making of* Malcolm X. New York: Hyperion, 1992, p. 7.

48. Quoted in Jones, *Spike Lee and the African American Filmmakers*, p. 78.

49. Quoted in Clarke, *Take a Lesson*, p. 107.

50. Quoted in Janice Mosier Richolson, "He's Gotta Have It: Interview with Spike Lee," in *Spike Lee: Interviews*, edited by Cynthia Fuchs. Jackson: University of Mississippi Press, 2002, p. 31.

51. Quoted in Emery, *The Directors*, p. 143.

52. Quoted in Marlaine Glicksman, "Spike Lee's Bed-Stuy BBQ," in *Spike Lee: Interviews*, p. 13.

53. Quoted in Emery, *The Directors*, p. 145.

54. Quoted in Glicksman, "Spike Lee's Bed-Stuy BBQ," p. 19.

55. Quoted in Emery, *The Directors*, p. 150.

56. Quoted in Richolson, "He's Gotta Have It," p. 29.

57. Quoted in Jones, *Spike Lee and the African American Filmmakers*, p. 95.

58. Quoted in Emery, *The Directors*, p. 152.

59. Quoted in Clarke, *Take a Lesson*, p. 109.

60. Quoted in Breskin, *Inner Views*, p. 188.

61. Quoted in Richolson, "He's Gotta Have It," p. 26.

62. Quoted in Clarke, *Take a Lesson*, p. 111.

Chapter 5: Peter Jackson

63. Quoted in Paul Lieberman, "Movies; 'Rings' Master; Director Peter Jackson Discusses His Seven Years on the Tolkien Trilogy," *Los Angeles Times*, December 19, 2003, p. E28.

64. Quoted in Gavin Edwards, "Lord of the Oscars," *Rolling Stone*, March 4, 2004, p. 32.

65. Quoted in Jay Carr, "Peter Jackson Stays Home," *Boston Globe*, July 14, 1996, p. B27.

66. Quoted in Carr, "Peter Jackson Stays Home," p. B27.

67. Quoted in Lieberman, "Movies; 'Rings' Master," p. E28.

68. Quoted in Andrew Johnston, "Not So Long Ago, 'a New Zealand Film' Didn't Even Exist," *New York Times*, February 4, 2001, p. 2.

69. Quoted in Stephen Rebello, "Peter Jackson's 'Bad Taste.'" *Variety*, December 2003/January 2004, p. 92.

70. Quoted in Julian Borger, "Tolkien Trilogy Director Rings Up $20m to Remake *King Kong*," *Guardian Manchester* (UK), August 13, 2003, p. 13.

71. Quoted in Johnston, "Not So Long Ago," p. 11.

72. Quoted in Steven Whitty, "New Zealand Horror-Flick Director Says He Tried to Tone Down the Gore," *Seattle Times*, July 19, 1996, p. F1.

73. Quoted in Whitty, "New Zealand Horror-Flick Director," p. F1.

74. Quoted in Gillian Flynn, "Gory Days," *Entertainment Weekly*, March 22, 2002, p. 63.

75. Quoted in Johnston, "Not So Long Ago," p. 2.

76. Quoted in Hal Hinson, "A Fright to Remember: Splatter Flick Director Has Personal Ghost Story," *Washington Post*, July 28, 1992, p. G2.

77. Quoted in Flynn, "Gory Days," p. 63.

78. Quoted in Carr, "Peter Jackson Stays Home," p. B27.

79. Quoted in Hinson, "A Fright to Remember," p. G2

80. Quoted in Hinson, "A Fright to Remember," p. G2.

81. Quoted in Stephen Galloway, "Dialogue with Peter Jackson," *Hollywood Reporter*, January 9, 2003, p. S8.

82. Quoted in Edwards, "Lord of the Oscars," p. 33.

83. Quoted in Laura Landro, "'The George Lucas of Christchurch'— How One Man Plans to Film Tolkien's Classic Trilogy in One Fell Swoop," *Wall Street Journal*, Eastern ed., December 1, 1999, p. A24.

84. Quoted in Landro, "'The George Lucas of Christchurch,'" p. A24.

85. Quoted in Lieberman, "Movies; 'Rings' Master," p. E28.

86. Quoted in Lieberman, "Movies; 'Rings' Master," p. E28.

87. Quoted in Edwards, "Lord of the Oscars," p. 33.

88. Quoted in Stephen Schaefer, "Lord of the Epic; 'Rings' Director Peter Jackson Works His Magic Through Patience," *Boston Herald*, December 16, 2002, p. 031.

89. Quoted in Schaefer, "Lord of the Epic," p. 031.

90. Quoted in Lieberman, "Movies; 'Rings' Master," p. E28.

91. Quoted in Edwards, "Lord of the Oscars," p. 33.

92. Quoted in Galloway, "Dialogue with Peter Jackson," p. S8.

93. Quoted in Galloway, "Dialogue with Peter Jackson," p. S8.

FOR FURTHER READING

Books

Bob Bernotas, *People to Know: Spike Lee: Filmmaker*. Hillsdale, NJ: Enslow, 1993. This young-adult biography covers the life and career of Spike Lee from birth through the time of the release of his film *Malcolm X*. Includes a few black-and-white photos, a chronology, and a filmography, as well as suggestions for further reading.

Karl French, *Karl French on* Apocalypse Now. New York: Bloomsbury, 1998. A thorough study of *Apocalypse Now* including its history, production, symbology, characters, and actors, arranged alphabetically for reference.

Ryan Gilbey, *It Don't Worry Me: The Revolutionary American Films of the Seventies*. New York: Faber and Faber, 2003. This collection includes essays on Francis Ford Coppola, Stanley Kubrick, and several other directors of significance to the 1970s.

Michael Herr, *Kubrick*. New York: Grove, 2000. This memoir, written by Kubrick's cowriter of the screenplay of *Full Metal Jacket*, provides insight into Kubrick's life, particularly his relationship with writers, actors, and other filmmaking colleagues.

Norman Kagan, *The Cinema of Stanley Kubrick*. New York: Holt, Rinehart and Winston, 1972. This book discusses each of Kubrick's films through *A Clockwork Orange*, including detailed synopses of plot, with short analyses of themes or topics at the end of each chapter.

Steven Kolpan, *A Sense of Place: An Intimate Portrait of the Niebaum-Coppola Winery and the Napa Valley*. New York: Routledge, 1999. A historic account of the winery and estate that Coppola purchased and revived.

Melissa McDaniel, *Book Report Biographies: Spike Lee: On His Own Terms*. Danbury, CT: Franklin Watts, 1998. This short biography for young readers covers Spike Lee's life and career through the time of his 1998 film *He Got Game*. Includes a chronology, a filmography, and a selection of sources for further reading.

Frederic Raphael, *Eyes Wide Open: A Memoir of Stanley Kubrick*. New York: Ballantine, 1999. This short memoir covers the author's relationship and experience working with Kubrick on the screenplay of *Eyes Wide Shut*. Provides insight into the director's personality and working style toward the end of his life.

Donald Spoto, *The Dark Side of Genius: The Life of Alfred Hitchcock*. New York: Little, Brown, 1983. This in-depth biography of the director focuses on the psychological factors in Hitchcock's life, which the author contends are in part responsible for the director's genius for macabre themes.

François Truffaut, *Hitchcock*. New York: Simon and Schuster, 1983. Documents the often-referenced interview between Hitchcock and French filmmaker/critic François Truffaut, including publicity pictures taken during the interview.

Web Sites

American Zoetrope (www.zoetrope.com). This Web site provides information on Francis Ford Coppola's companies, including his literary magazine *Zoetrope All-Story* and his winery. Also includes Coppola-related historical and biographical information, news, and other features.

Authorized Stanley Kubrick Web Site (http://kubrickfilms.warner bros.com/mainmenu/mainmenu.html). This fan site includes biographical information, a complete filmography, news, FAQs, message boards, and other special features.

The Bastards Have Landed: The Official Peter Jackson Fan Club (http://tbhl.theonering.net/index.shtml). This Web site provides biographical information, filmography, fan message boards, merchandise, and news about Jackson and his films.

Internet Movie Database (www.imdb.com). This Web site provides biographical information on filmmakers and other celebrities. Includes filmographies and trivia information for each person.

Mystery.Net's Alfred Hitchcock Site (www.mysterynet.com/hitchcock). This Web site includes biographical information and links to information about Hitchcock's films, television programs, and interviews with people he worked with.

WORKS CONSULTED

Books

Gene Adair, *Alfred Hitchcock: Filming Our Fears.* New York: Oxford University Press, 2003. This short, readable volume covers the highlights of Hitchcock's life and career and includes several black-and-white photographs. Also includes a chronology and filmography.

John Baxter, *Stanley Kubrick: A Biography.* New York: Carroll & Graf, 1997. This biography follows Kubrick's life from birth to 1997, when the director was working on his last film.

David Breskin, *Inner Views: Filmmakers in Conversation.* New York: Da Capo, 1997. A collection of interviews with eight directors, with interviews between the author and Coppola and Spike Lee.

Jeffrey Chown, *Hollywood Auteur: Francis Coppola.* New York: Praeger, 1988. This volume follows Coppola's career from his first film to the late 1980s, dealing in detail with the financial troubles the director experienced while attempting to create films that were both personally interesting and commercially viable.

Michel Ciment, *Kubrick: The Definitive Edition.* New York: Faber and Faber, 2001. This in-depth pictorial biography and examination of Kubrick's life and work includes numerous photos and film stills, as well as interviews from actors, writers, and others who worked with and knew Kubrick. Includes a filmography and a chronology.

Caroline V. Clarke, *Take a Lesson: Today's Black Achievers on How They Made It and What They Learned Along the Way.* New York: John Wiley & Sons, 2001. This book contains first-person accounts by prominent African American figures, including Spike Lee, focusing on their life and achievements.

Paul Duncan, *Stanley Kubrick: His Complete Films.* Koln, Germany: Tachen, 2003. This study of Kubrick's work includes numerous color and black-and-white photos, both from Kubrick's films and from those taken during the making of the films. Also includes discussion of each of the films' plots and themes and biographical information on Kubrick throughout.

Robert J. Emery, *The Directors: Take One.* New York: TV, 1999. This collection of thirteen essays includes interview materials and commentaries on films by the directors. Contains an interview with Spike Lee.

Cynthia Fuchs, ed., *Spike Lee: Interviews.* Jackson: University of Mississippi Press, 2002. This collection of twenty-two interviews spans from 1986, shortly after the release of *Do the Right*

Thing, to 2002. Includes a chronology of Lee's life and career and a filmography.

Sidney Gottlieb, ed., *Alfred Hitchcock Interviews*. Jackson: University of Mississippi Press, 2003. This collection of twenty interviews covers the scope of Hitchcock's career from his first arrival in the United States.

————, ed., *Hitchcock on Hitchcock: Selected Writings and Interviews*. Berkeley: University of California Press, 1995. This collection of essays by Hitchcock discusses his life and career and includes a discussion of the themes of his work.

K. Maurice Jones, *Spike Lee and the African American Filmmakers: A Choice of Colors*. Brookfield, CT: Millbrook, 1996. This volume provides a history of African Americans in filmmaking, focusing on the life and career of Spike Lee.

Christiane Kubrick, *Stanley Kubrick: A Life in Pictures*. Boston: Bulfinch, a 2002. This pictorial study, assembled and annotated by Kubrick's third wife, includes many heretofore unpublished pictures of Kubrick at work, along with family, colleagues, and friends. Includes a filmography and a chronology.

Harlan Lebo, *The Godfather Legacy*. New York: Fireside, 1997. This book covers the history of the making of the three *Godfather* films, as well as plot and descriptions, dialogue excerpts, photos of the making of the films, and film stills.

Spike Lee, Terry McMillan, and David Lee, *Five for Five: The Films of Spike Lee*. New York: Stewart, Tabori & Chang, 1991. This essay and photo collection focuses on Lee's five features: *She's Gotta Have It, School Daze, Do the Right Thing, Mo' Better Blues,* and *Jungle Fever*. Includes a foreword by Melvin Van Peebles.

Spike Lee, with Ralph Wiley, *By Any Means Necessary: The Trials and Tribulations of the Making of* Malcolm X. New York: Hyperion, 1992. Spike Lee's detailed account of the making of *Malcolm X*. Includes the full screenplay.

Jon Lewis, *Whom God Wishes to Destroy: Francis Coppola and the New Hollywood*. Durham, NC: Duke University Press, 1995. This biographical study follows Coppola and his films, focusing on the financial risks, fiascos, and successes of his career.

Vincent LoBrutto, *Stanley Kubrick: A Biography*. New York: Donald I. Fine, 1997. This biography follows the life of Stanley Kubrick, including details of his parents' and grandparents' lives, through 1997 when Kubrick was at work on his last film, *Eyes Wide Shut*. Includes a section of black-and-white photographs, some of which were taken by Kubrick as a young photographer.

Patrick McGilligan, *Alfred Hitchcock: A Life in Darkness and Light*. New York: Regan, 2003. This lengthy, detailed, and authoritative biography covers Hitchcock's life, career, and legacy, and also works to sort the facts of Hitchcock's life from the numerous rumors that have circulated for decades.

Ken Mog, *The Alfred Hitchcock Story*. Dallas: Taylor, 1999. This pictorial biography includes numerous color and black-and-white photos, including an excellent selection of biographical shots, film stills, behind-the-scenes shots of Hitchcock at work, and reproductions of film posters.

Gene Phillips, ed., *Alfred Hitchcock*. Boston: G.K. Hall, 1984. This book of essays discusses each of Hitchcock's films, including a plot synopsis and a brief discussion of themes. Also includes a complete filmography of Hitchcock's films.

——, *Stanley Kubrick: Interviews*. Jackson: University of Mississippi Press, 2001. This collection of sixteen interviews was assembled from various publications from 1959 to 1987. Includes a filmography and a chronology.

Ian Pryor, *Peter Jackson: From Prince of Splatter to Lord of the Rings*. New York: Thomas Dunne, 2004. The first full-length biography of Jackson, covering his life through the release of the third *The Lord of the Rings* film, *The Fellowship of the Ring*. Appendices provide a Jackson time line, a filmography, and a listing of his inspirations and influences.

Steven Jay Schneider, ed. *1001 Movies You Must See Before You Die*. London: Quintet, 2003. This book is an excellent reference of great films selected by the authors and chronologically arranged. Each listing includes a critical review, information about the film, and a full-color still taken from the film.

Michael Schumacher, *Francis Ford Coppola: A Filmmaker's Life*. New York: Crown, 1999. An in-depth biography of Francis Ford Coppola, from his birth to his work and activities of the late 1990s. Includes a filmography.

John Russell Taylor, *Hitch: The Life and Times of Alfred Hitchcock*. London: Faber and Faber, 1978. The first authorized biography of Hitchcock and considered by other biographers as one of the most authoritative, Taylor's book covers Hitchock's life and career through the late 1970s, shortly before the director's death.

Peter Travers, ed., *The Rolling Stone Film Reader: The Best Film Writing from* Rolling Stone *Magazine*. New York: Pocket, 1996. This volume contains an excellent collection of film essays and interviews published by *Rolling Stone* magazine since the magazine's debut in 1967. Includes material on Stanley Kubrick and Francis Ford Coppola.

Periodicals

Ad Media, "Jackson Keen to Make Kiwi Movies," December 2003.

———, "Miramar Mogul: An Exclusive Interview with Peter Jackson," December 2003.

Julian Borger, "Tolkien Trilogy Director Rings Up $20m to Remake *King Kong*," *Guardian Manchester* (UK), August 13, 2003.

Tim Cahill, "Stanley Kubrick" (interview), *Rolling Stone*, August 27, 1987.

Jay Carr, "Peter Jackson Stays Home," *Boston Globe*, July 14, 1996.

Gavin Edwards, "Lord of the Oscars," *Rolling Stone*, March 4, 2004.

Gillian Flynn, "Gory Days," *Entertainment Weekly*, March 22, 2002.

Stephen Galloway, "Dialogue with Peter Jackson," *Hollywood Reporter*, January 9, 2003.

Hal Hinson, "A Fright to Remember: Splatter Flick Director Has Personal Ghost Story," *Washington Post*, July 28, 1992.

Hollywood Reporter, "Dialogue," February 27, 2003.

Andrew Johnston, "Not So Long Ago, 'a New Zealand Film' Didn't Even Exist," *New York Times*, February 4, 2001.

Laura Landro, "'The George Lucas of Christchurch'—How One Man Plans to Film Tolkien's Classic Trilogy in One Fell Swoop," *Wall Street Journal*, Eastern ed., December 1, 1999.

Paul Lieberman, "Movies; 'Rings' Master; Director Peter Jackson Discusses His Seven Years on the Tolkien Trilogy," *Los Angeles Times*, December 19, 2003.

Stephen Rebello, "Peter Jackson's 'Bad Taste,'" *Variety*, December 2003/January 2004.

Stephen Schaefer, "Lord of the Epic; 'Rings' Director Peter Jackson Works His Magic Through Patience," *Boston Herald*, December 16, 2002.

Steven Whitty, "New Zealand Horror-Flick Director Says He Tried to Tone Down the Gore," *Seattle Times*, July 19, 1996.

INDEX

Picture Credits

About the Author

Andy Koopmans is the author of ten books, including biographies of Bruce Lee, Madonna, the Osbournes, Charles Lindbergh, Pol Pot, and Nelson Mandela. He is also a fiction writer, essayist, poet, and avid cineast. He saw Kubrick's *2001: A Space Odyssey* when he was eight months old and has never been the same. He lives in Seattle, Washington, with his wife, Angela Mihm, and their pets Bubz, Licorice, and Zachary. He would like to thank the staff at Lucent Books, particularly Jennifer Skancke and Chandra Howard, for their assistance in preparing this book for publication.